TRUTH
OF THE
MATTER

ANSWERING QUESTIONS WITH SCRIPTURES

RUSSELL N. GREINER

CFI

AN IMPRINT OF CEDAR FORT, INC.
SPRINGVILLE, UTAH

I have known Russ Greiner for over forty years. We even taught on the same faculty for a short time. He is a Christ-centered, scripture-based teacher. Because of his diligent study and memorization of the scriptures and words of apostles and prophets, he has often been invited to represent the Church before universities, high schools, and private Christian and Catholic schools and serve on panels with other religious leaders. Russ has a unique ability to answer people's questions with scripture in a practical, non-offensive manner. This book will help the reader do the same and become a valiant defender of the faith in an uncertain world.

—JACK R. CHRISTIANSON
Retired religious educator, best-selling author

ISBN 13: 978-1-4621-4371-9

Published by CFI, an imprint of Cedar Fort, Inc.
2373 W. 700 S., Springville, UT 84663
Distributed by Cedar Fort, Inc., www.cedarfort.com

Library of Congress Control Number: 2022945330

Cover design by Courtney Proby
Cover design © 2022 Cedar Fort, Inc.

Printed in the United States of America

10 9 8 7 6 5 4 3 2 1

Printed on acid-free paper

Contents

Introduction 1

1. Are you Mormon? 2

2. If you have something better, I will go to church with you.....................3

3. Two minutes and fifty-seven seconds to distinguish the Church from all other churches and world religions 5

4. How do you justify latter-day prophets and scripture, angels and visions, polygamy, becoming a god, and a Heavenly Mother? 7

5. We have the Bible. Why do we need Joseph Smith? 15

6. Are Mormons Christian?.. 17

7. What is the role of women in your church? 20

8. What is your position on same-sex marriage?..................................21

9. You cannot destroy the truth by refusing to accept it 23

10. Why isn't the Book of Mormon mentioned in the Bible? 25

11. Isn't 1 Corinthians 15:29 about baptism for the dead simply a rhetorical question? The Bible is inerrant! How do you justify your eighth article of faith? 35

12. The prophet Isaiah taught, "Before me there was no God." Therefore, Mormon doctrine that man can become a god must be false! 38

13. "Ye shall know them by their fruits" 39

14. Do you know how The Church of Jesus Christ of Latter-day Saints began? 43

15. It does make a difference which church you belong to 45

16. Mormons believe they can work their way to heaven 47

17. I'm an atheist—convince me! 49

18. "I am a child of God" is merely a feel-good idea 52

19. Where did you gentlemen get the authority to organize a church in our town? 54

20. The holy garments of salvation 56

21. When I go on vacation, will you be the minister for the day to my Unitarian congregation? 57

22. I don't need Joseph Smith and his successors. All I need is in the Bible. 60

23. Joseph Smith's prophecy that the New Jerusalem temple would be reared in this generation was not fulfilled. Doesn't this expose him as a false prophet? Hasn't modern DNA research proved that the Book of Mormon is false? 62

24. "Now I know what hell would be like" 72

25. When you see the wounds in the Savior's hands, what will you say to Him then? 74

26. The law of tithing specifies a particularly profound, prophetic promise 76

27. We have come to listen to a prophet's voice and hear the word of God 77

28. Why do you reject the creeds when they are clearly taught in the Bible and Book of Mormon? 78

29. Some people believe Mormonism is a cult 81

30. Who will accept our message? 84

31. The Book of Mormon is an addition to the Bible. Therefore, you are accursed! 87

32. The Bible is scripture that teaches Christian principles. What is the purpose of the Book of Mormon? 88

33. "My father taught that missionary work brings a remission of sins" 91

34. "Tell her you're a member of the Church!" 94

35. If I knew there is a living prophet on the earth today, no storm, barking dog, amount of rejection, or sacrifice could deter me from declaring our message 95

36. The conversion of the Prince of Chad could impact his entire nation 98

37. The Spirit said, "Slow down!" 100

38. Have you heard of the Word of Wisdom? 103

39. "The Spirit directed us to your home!" 106

40. "How great shall be your joy!" 108

41. Immediately following the priesthood blessing he came out of his coma 109

42. His faith is sufficient to be healed 111

43. Dinner with a dead guy 114

44. Ten reasons I joined The Church of Jesus Christ of Latter-day Saints 116

45. If you live it, you'll be happy; if you don't, you won't 121

46. I had a mother who read the Bible to me 123

47. "Elder Sill, what is your key to success?" 127

48. Memorize one scripture a week 128

49. My testimony 132

Russell N. Greiner, CES Institute Director, Memorized Scripture List 133

About the Author 140

Introduction

The minister of a Christian school asked me to explain to his students how I, an evangelical Christian, who attended a Baptist college, and participated in Campus Crusade for Christ, was baptized into The Church of Jesus Christ of Latter-day Saints. During my thirty-year career teaching seminary and institute, I have been invited more than forty times to represent the Church at various high schools, universities, and before an audience with other religious leaders to explain our beliefs. I have taken 1 Peter 3:15 seriously: "Be ready always to give an answer to every man that asketh you a reason of the hope that is in you."

Elder Neal A. Maxwell taught, "Holy Scripture and the words of living prophets occupy a privileged position: they are the key to teaching by the spirit so that we communicate in what the Prophet Joseph Smith called "the language of inspiration."[1] Accordingly, I have committed to memory more than 3,000 verses of scripture and inspirational quotations. At the end of this book is my memorized scripture list. Thousands of my mission prep students have taken this document into the mission field so these powerful references by topic are at their fingertips.

The stories in this book illustrate that the answers to your questions are found in the scriptures. It is my hope that the readers of this book will use this information to more effectively share the truths of the gospel.

---

1. Neal A. Maxwell, "Teaching by the Spirit—'The language of Inspiration,'" *Old Testament Symposium Speeches*, 1991.

1

Are you Mormon?

The First Presidency has reminded us to use the full name of the Church rather than the nickname Mormon. Doctrine and Covenants 115:4 states, "For thus shall my church be called in the last days, even The Church of Jesus Christ of Latter-day Saints."

I have been asked on numerous occasions, "Are you Mormon?" Occasionally, I reply, "Thanks for the compliment. Mormon means 'more good.'[2] Mormon was a prophet, an author, and the last Nephite military commander (310–385 AD). The Book of Mormon bears his name because he was the major abridger of the gold plates from which it was translated. He was a 'sober child' and 'quick to observe' and in his fifteenth year 'was visited of the Lord' (see Mormon 1:2, 15). At age sixteen he became the general of all the Nephite armies (see Mormon 2:2). Before his death, he delivered the records entrusted to him to his son, Moroni, who buried them in the Hill Cumorah. No, I am not Mormon, but I am a member of The Church of Jesus Christ of Latter-day Saints."

---

2. Joseph Fielding Smith, *Teachings of the Prophet Joseph Smith*, 300.

2

If you have something better,
I will go to church with you

I grew up in Arcadia, California, and was blessed to have exceptional friends. We did everything together except date each other's girlfriends.

I joined The Church of Jesus Christ of Latter-day Saints at Brigham Young University. Two weeks later my friends and I returned home from college and decided to have a reunion in Huntington Beach, California, at lifeguard tower number seven. About twenty of us attended the event and were catching up with each other when my buddy Scott blurted out, "Hey, Greiner, I heard you are a Mormon."

I answered, "True blue, through and through!"

The other guys heard this startling news and gathered around to learn more.

Scott continued, "Maybe if you came with me to the Methodist church you would be a Methodist now instead of a Mormon."

I testified, "If you have something better than God the Eternal Father and His Son Jesus Christ appearing to Joseph Smith and calling him to be a prophet to end the Dark Ages and Reformation Era and usher in the dispensation of the fulness of times. If you have something better than the Angel Moroni directing Joseph Smith to the gold plates, which he translated by the gift and power of God into the Book of Mormon—Another Testament of Jesus Christ, in fulfillment of Revelation 14:6: 'And I saw another angel fly in the midst of heaven, having the everlasting gospel to preach unto them that dwell on the earth, and to every nation, and kindred, and tongue, and people.' If you have something better than John the Baptist, the same man who had baptized the Savior, restore the Aaronic Priesthood to Joseph Smith and Oliver Cowdery. If you have something better than Peter, James, and John, Christ's three main apostles, restore the Melchizedek Priesthood. If you have something better than Moses restoring the keys of the gathering of Israel, and Elias committing the dispensation of the gospel of Abraham. If you have something better than Elijah restoring the sealing keys to bind on earth and seal in heaven so our temple marriages can be for time and eternity rather than 'until death do you part' in fulfillment of Malachi 4:5–6: 'Behold, I will send you Elijah the prophet before the coming of the great and dreadful day of the Lord. And he shall turn the heart of the fathers to the children and the heart of the children to their fathers, lest I come and smite the earth with a curse.'"

I ended, "If you have something better than that, I will go to church with you on Sunday. But if not, why don't you come with me?"

Standing next to me was my friend Clark. He heard my testimony and joined the Church three months later. Several years ago, I was invited to speak at a tri-stake youth conference in Los Angeles, California. Who do you suppose was presiding as a member of the stake presidency? Yes, it was my high school friend Clark. The Lord has promised, "Open your mouths and they shall be filled" (D&C 33:7–10). Testify of so glorious a message!

3

Two minutes and fifty-seven seconds to distinguish the Church from all other churches and world religions

Over the years I have been given the opportunity to represent the Church to groups not of our faith more than forty times. I participated on a panel of ministers at the University of California–Irvine. I know this sounds like a lead in to a joke, but the group consisted of a Buddhist, Muslim, Sikh, Jewish Rabbi, Evangelical Christian, Catholic Priest, and Latter-day Saint. The moderator was a Unitarian. The first forty-five-minute segment was called a "Fish Bowl." The audience watched the moderator ask us searching questions, and we each had three minutes to answer. The second half allowed the audience to ask us any question on any subject they desired. To be prepared to answer any and every question imaginable is an awesome undertaking.

We began the presentation with a three-minute introduction of ourselves and our organization. I said, "My name is Russ Greiner. I am an ordained bishop in The Church of Jesus Christ of Latter-day Saints." This left me two minutes and fifty-seven seconds to introduce the Church and distinguish our faith from the other churches and world religions.

I commenced by quoting Joseph Fielding Smith: "No man of himself can lead this church. It is the Church of the Lord Jesus Christ; He is at the head. The Church bears his name, has his priesthood, administers his gospel, preaches his doctrine, and does his work. He chooses [people] and calls them to be instruments in his hands to accomplish his purposes, and he guides and directs them in their labors [by revelation]."[3]

I then said, "Let's examine how the Savior directed His Church after His resurrection. The book of Acts begins with these words: 'The former treatise have I made, O Theophilus, of all that Jesus began

---

3. Joseph Fielding Smith, *Improvement Era*, June 1970, 26.

both to do and teach. Until the day in which he was taken up, after that he through the Holy Ghost had given commandments unto the apostles whom he had chosen' (Acts 1:1–2). Christ directed His ancient Church by revelation through his chosen servants, the apostles."

Next, I recited John Taylor's statement: "Adam's revelations did not instruct Noah to build his ark; nor did Noah's revelations tell Lot to forsake Sodom; nor did either of these speak of the departure of the children of Israel from Egypt. These all had revelations for themselves, and so had Isaiah, Jeremiah, Ezekiel, Jesus, Peter, Paul, John, and Joseph. And so must we."[4]

I told them of Rufus Jones, a Quaker teacher and writer, who said, "Vital religion cannot be maintained and preserved on the theory that God dealt with our human race only in the far past ages, and that the Bible is the only evidence we have that our God is a living, revealing, communicating God. If God ever spoke, He is still speaking. He is the great I Am, not the great He Was!"[5]

I inquired, "Does God not love us as much as those He directed by ancient prophets? Don't we need His inspired guidance today? Has God lost His voice, or does He not care about us? Has He gone on an extended vacation, or is He asleep?"

I concluded with Amos 3:7: "Surely the Lord God will do nothing, but he revealeth his secret unto his servants the prophets."

I testified, "The Church of Jesus Christ of Latter-day Saints is distinct from all other churches and world religions because we have a living prophet of God on the earth today who speaks the mind, and word, and is the voice of the Lord. The Church is directed in latter days as it was in former times, by revelation through living prophets."

The Evangelical Christian exhaled quite loudly. Another panelist said, "Good answer." The next minister in sequence began by saying, "How do I follow that?" I have thought since, "This is the greatest message in the world since Christ rose from the grave and ascended into heaven! How do you follow that?"

---

4. John Taylor, *The Gospel Kingdom*, 34.
5. Rufus Jones, "A Flash of Eternity," *Ensign*, November 1992, 63.

4

How do you justify latter-day prophets and scripture, angels and visions, polygamy, becoming a god, and a Heavenly Mother?

I was invited to share our beliefs at a private Christian school in Southern California. Their minister asked me to teach his high school students for thirty minutes and answer questions for twenty minutes. However, when school ended at 3:00 p.m., the entire class remained in their seats for an additional hour asking questions.

After I explained the Joseph Smith story and First Vision, a student raised his hand and declared, "The Bible shows that God spoke anciently through prophets, and then He spoke to us through Christ, and that there will be no more prophets."

I inquired, "Are you referring to Hebrews 1:1–2?"

He answered, "Yes."

I recited these verses: "God, who at sundry times and in diverse manners spake in time past unto the fathers by the prophets, Hath in these last days spoken unto us by his Son, whom he hath appointed heir of all things." I pointed out, "Nowhere in these verses or in the entire Bible does it state that God will discontinue speaking to his children through prophets." I asked, "Do you believe the Bible to be the word of God?"

He proclaimed emphatically, "Absolutely!"

"Who do you believe wrote the book of Hebrews?"

He answered, "The Apostle Paul."

I inquired, "Did Paul know Jesus during His mortal ministry?"

He admitted, "No."

I then asked, "Did Paul know Jesus during the forty days He tarried in Jerusalem after His resurrection?"

He again stated, "No."

I asked, "How, then, did Paul qualify to be an apostle?"

The student replied, "The Lord appeared to Paul on the road to Damascus and called him to the ministry."

I then said, "That is correct. In 1 Corinthians 9:1, Paul states, 'Am I not an apostle? . . . Have I not seen Jesus Christ our Lord?'" I continued, "So, if I understand you correctly, you are saying that after Christ atoned for our sins, was crucified, died on the cross, was buried, rose from the grave, and ascended into heaven, He appeared to and called Paul to be an apostle? Paul then wrote fourteen books of the New Testament."

He declared with conviction, "Yes!"

I testified, "Likewise, after Christ atoned for our sins, was crucified, died on the cross, was buried, rose from the grave, and ascended into heaven, He appeared to and called Joseph Smith to be a latter-day prophet. 'The Lord who spoke to His servant Paul on the road to Damascus is the same one who spoke to His servant Joseph in [Palmyra].'[6] Joseph Smith brought forth more scripture than the twelve most prophetic prolific penmen of the past combined. Paul received priesthood authority from the living apostles (see Acts 13:2–3). Joseph Smith received priesthood authority from Peter, James, and John (see Doctrine and Covenants 27:12–13). With that priesthood authority, Paul and Joseph performed miracles in the name of the Lord, including raising the dead. Both enjoyed the ministering of angels, prophesied, had visions, and sealed their testimonies of Christ with their own blood." I inquired of the group, "How can anyone accept Paul as an apostle and not accept Joseph Smith as a prophet for the exact same reasons?"

The second question was, "We respect the Mormon people, but what about those angels and visions Joseph Smith claimed to see?" As you can see by the way he worded his question, he was attempting to put me on the defensive. I teach my mission prep students to take their investigators questions and turn them around to offense, and my answer is the reason they should join the Church.

I explained, "Were there not angels and visions in Christ's Church in the New Testament? Did not an angel appear to Zacharias, the father of John the Baptist? Did not an angel appear to Mary in Luke chapter 1? Did not angels appear to Peter, James, and John on the Mount of Transfiguration? Did not an angel rescue Peter and John from prison? Did not an angel appear to Cornelius? Did not an angel

---

6. Brad Wilcox, *Because of the Messiah in a Manger*, 101.

appear to Paul before his shipwreck and John on the Isle of Patmos? Did not Peter have a vision of the gospel going to the Gentiles in Acts 10? Did not Paul have a vision of the three degrees of glory in 1 Corinthians 15? Is not the book of Revelation a compilation of visions given to John of the latter days (see Revelation 4:1)? Did not Stephen have a vision in Acts 7 of Jesus standing on the right hand of God as did Joseph Smith? (Joseph Smith–History 1:16–17). Yes, Joseph Smith enjoyed the ministering of angels and saw glorious visions, because he was the instrument in the hands of God to restore the same Church that Christ established when He was on the earth."

In attendance, observing the class, was a teacher from a Christian high school in Rancho Bernardo, California. She asked two questions: First, "How do Mormons justify polygamy?" I recited a statement I memorized on my mission:

> Why do people honor the laws of the polygamist Moses,
> Bask in the wisdom of the polygamist Solomon,
> Sing of the songs of the polygamist David,
> Pray to enter the gate of the city wherein are written the names of
> the 12 polygamous sons of the polygamist Jacob,
> Go to the bosom of the polygamist Abraham,
> Then curse the polygamist Brigham Young?[7]

The Prophet Joseph Smith declared, "I hold the keys of this power in the last days; for there is never but one on earth at a time on whom the power and its keys are conferred; and I have constantly said no man shall have but one wife at a time, unless the Lord directs otherwise."[8]

I continued, "There are two reasons stated for the practice of plural marriage in the Book of Mormon. Jacob 2:28–30 says, 'For I, the Lord God, delight in the chastity of women. And whoredoms are an abomination before me. . . . Wherefore, this people shall keep my commandments . . . or cursed be the land for their sakes. For if I will, saith the Lord of Hosts, raise up seed unto me, I will command my people; otherwise, they shall hearken unto these things.' Therefore, if the Lord commands it or to raise up seed (multiple and replenish), he will initiate plural marriage. A third reason was explained by Elder Orson Pratt: 'The Church as

---

7. Author unknown.
8. Joseph Fielding Smith, *Teachings of the Prophet Joseph Smith*, 324.

heir of the keys required anciently for plural marriages to be sanctioned by God, was required to perform such marriages as part of the restoration."[9]

In 1890, the Church ended the practice of plural marriage by revelation to the Prophet Wilford Woodruff who explained,

> I saw by the inspiration of Almighty God what lay before this people, and I knew that something had to be done to ward off the blow that was impending. But I should have let come to pass what God showed me by revelation and vision; I should have lived in the flesh and permitted these things to come to pass; I should have let this temple go into the hands of our enemies; I should have let every temple be confiscated by the hands of the wicked; I should have permitted our personal property to have been confiscated by our enemies; I should have seen this people—prophets and apostles, driven by the hands of their enemies, and our wives and children scattered to the four winds of heaven—I should have seen all this, had not Almighty God commanded me to do what I did.[10]

I completed my answer to this question by asking the teachers and students two questions: "Was not the whole house of Israel built on the twelve sons of Jacob, who had four wives?" (See Genesis 29:23, 28; Genesis 30:4, 9). And, "If the practice of plural marriage is an abomination to God, then why does the Lord declare that the polygamist prophets Abraham, Isaac, and Jacob have entered into the kingdom of heaven?" (See Matthew 8:11.) They had no response.

The teacher's second question was, "Will you come to my Christian high school in Rancho Bernardo, California, and speak to my students?" I readily agreed with a smile.

Another student pointed at me and asked sarcastically, "Do you believe you will become a god?" It would be quite presumptuous to simply say yes. So, I began by explaining that we believe in the law of eternal progression and forever is a long time. I then quoted my favorite eternity poem:

> In the land of Oden, there stands a mountain 10,000 miles in the air.
> From edge to edge this mountain, 10,000 miles square.

---

9. *Encyclopedia of Mormonism*, 3:1094. See also Acts 3:20–21.
10. See Mark E. Petersen, *The Way of the Master* (Salt Lake City: Bookcraft, 1974), 50–52.

A little bird comes winging once every million years,
And sharpens its beak on that mountain, then swiftly disappears.
Thus, when that mountain is slowly worn away—
This to Eternity will be but one single day.[11]

I recited the inspired teaching of President Joseph Fielding Smith: "Man is the child of God, formed in the divine image and endowed with divine attributes, and even as the infant son of an earthly father and mother is capable in due time of becoming a man, so the undeveloped offspring of celestial parentage is capable, by experience through the ages and eons, of evolving into a God."[12]

I continued, "Let's examine what the Bible teaches on this subject. Psalm 82:1 and 6 states, 'God standeth in the congregation of the mighty; he judgeth among the gods. I have said, Ye are gods; and all of you are children of the Most High.'" I inquired, "Wouldn't it be something if the Savior quoted this very verse during his mortal ministry?"

They shook their heads. "We know our Bible and there is no way that is in the New Testament!"

I invited them to read John 10:34–35: "Jesus answered them, is it not written in your law, I said, Ye are gods? If he called them gods, unto whom the word of God came, and the scripture cannot be broken."

I then directed them to Philippians 2:5–6: "Let this mind be in you, which was also in Christ Jesus: Who being in the form of God, thought it not robbery to be equal with God."

I explained that this is the mindset that Paul said we should all have. I shared with them the words of the early Christian fathers concerning godhood:

> Saint Irenaeus, the most important Christian theologian of his time, said, "Do we cast blame on him [God] because we were not made gods from the beginning, but were at first created merely as men, and then later as gods?'
>
> Saint Clement of Alexandria wrote, "Yea, I say, the Word of God became a man so that you might learn from a man how to become a god. If one knows himself, he will know God, and knowing God will

---

11. Ben Best, Song, "Land of Oden."
12. Joseph Fielding Smith, *Man: His Origin and Destiny*, 354–355.

become like God . . . His is beauty, true beauty, for it is God, and that man becomes a god, since God wills it."

Saint Justin Martyr [said], "[Men] were made like God . . . deemed worthy of becoming gods and of having power to become sons of the highest."

In the early fourth century Saint Athanasius after whom the orthodox Athanasian Creed is named stated, "The Word was made flesh in order that we might be enabled to be made gods . . . He became man that we might be made divine."

Saint Augustine himself, the greatest of the Christian Fathers, said, "But he himself that justifies also deifies, for by justifying he makes sons of God. For he has given them power to become the sons of God (John 1:12). If then we have been made sons of God, we have also been made gods."[13]

Next, we read under the topic of deification in *The Westminster Dictionary of Christian Theology*, which is found in theology schools across the country.

Deification (Greek theosis) is for Orthodoxy the goal of every Christian. Man, according to the Bible, is 'made in the image and likeness of God.' . . . It is possible for man to become like God, to become deified, to become god by grace. . . .

Finally, it should be noted that deification does not mean absorption into God, since the deified creature remains itself and distinct. It is the whole human being, body and soul, who is transfigured in the Spirit into the likeness of the divine nature, and deification is the goal of every Christian.[14]

We then discussed what C. S. Lewis, a Protestant thinker and writer, said in his book *Mere Christianity*:

The command, "Be ye perfect," is not idealistic gas. Nor is it a commandment to do the impossible. He is going to make us into creatures that can obey that command. He said (in the Bible) that we were "gods'" and He is going to make good His words. If we let Him—for we can prevent Him, if we choose—He will make the feeblest and filthiest of us into a god or goddess, dazzling, radiant,

13. Stephen E. Robinson, *Are Mormons Christians?*, 60–61.
14. *The Westminster Dictionary of Christian Theology*, 1983, 147–148.

immortal creatures, pulsating all through with such energy and joy and wisdom and love as we cannot now imagine. . . . The process will be long and in parts very painful; but that is what we are in for. Nothing less. He meant what He said.[15]

The teacher got up from his chair in the back of the room, walked to his desk, and examined his copy of *Mere Christianity* to verify that I didn't take this statement by C. S. Lewis out of context. After reading the quote he simply said, "Hmm."

The follow-up question was, "Did God have a father?" I quoted Revelation 1:6: "And hath made us kings and priests unto God and his Father; to him be glory and dominion for ever and ever. Amen." I added, "Where was there ever a son without a father? And where was there ever a father without first being a son? Hence, if Jesus had a father, can we not believe that His father had a father also?"[16]

Another question was, "How is it you believe in a Heavenly Mother?" I shared, "Latter-day Saints believe in continuous revelation through living prophets. In 1909 the First Presidency of the Church declared, 'All men and women are in the similitude of the universal Father and Mother, and are literally the sons and daughters of Deity.'"[17]

"The Prophet Spencer W. Kimball taught, 'God made man in his own image and certainly he made woman in the image of his wife-partner. . . . You [women] are daughters of God. You are precious. You are made in the image of our Heavenly Mother.'"[18]

In "The Family: A Proclamation to the World," we are told that "all human beings—male and female—are created in the image of God. Each is a beloved spirit son or daughter of heavenly parents, and, as such, each has a divine nature and destiny."

After an hour and fifty minutes a student made the perfect inquiry to finish our discussion: "What must a person do to become a member of your church?"

---

15. Ibid., 174–175.
16. Joseph Fielding Smith, *Teachings of the Prophet Joseph Smith*, 373.
17. *Messages of the First Presidency*, 4:203.
18. *The Teachings of Spencer W. Kimball*, 24–25.

Wow, was I glad to be asked that question! I said, "I extend to you the same invitation that Peter gave to disciples two thousand years ago on the day of Pentecost, when the spirit was poured out, and devout men out of every nation recognized the apostles as authorized representatives of the Lord Jesus Christ." I then quoted Acts 2:37–38: "'Now when they heard this, they were pricked in their heart, and said unto Peter and to the rest of the apostles, Men and brethren, what shall we do? Then Peter said unto them, Repent, and be baptized every one of you in the name of Jesus Christ for the remission of sins, and ye shall receive the gift of the Holy Ghost.'"

Their religion teacher said to his students, "Have we ever had a speaker that you wanted to stay for a full hour after school to listen to? Have we ever had a speaker that defended his doctrinal beliefs from the Bible as powerfully as did Mr. Greiner? Mr. Greiner really made us think today. Would you like to have him back?"

They replied in unison, "Yes!"

5

We have the Bible.
Why do we need Joseph Smith?

As Director of the Mission Viejo Institute of Religion, I went with about ten students and the missionaries down to Saddleback College for Club Rush. The clubs on campus set up booths to promote their organization and recruit members. Next to our table was the Bible Study Club. They kept staring at our display with copies of the Book of Mormon, Church literature, and Institute class schedules, and finally asked, "We have the Bible. Why do we need Joseph Smith?"

I testified, "Because there was not a man upon the earth who knew God other than by hearsay! Because the kingdom of God cannot be ruled by a book! (God sent Moses, not the Ten Commandments, to lead Israel.) Because the Church organized by Jesus Christ was not to be found anywhere upon the earth! Because the doctrines of salvation as taught by Christ and the ancient prophets had been lost or polluted with the philosophies of men! Because the authority of the priesthood had been taken from men."[19]

They countered with, "How do you know that Joseph Smith is a prophet?" I answered, "There is probably more evidence of his divine call and mission than of any other prophet who ever lived. Joseph Smith translated the Book of Mormon from ancient plates. Its purpose is to be another testament of Jesus Christ. He received and recorded the revelations in the Doctrine and Covenants and Pearl of Great Price. In so doing he brought forth more scripture than the twelve greatest writers of the Bible combined. Joseph Smith received the priesthood from Peter, James and John, Christ's three main apostles, and with that apostolic authority and as the authorized servant of God, re-established the Church of Jesus Christ. He restored all the doctrines, ordinances, covenants and the fulness of the gospel. He performed a host

---

19. "The Church and Kingdom of God," *Teachings of Presidents of the Church: Joseph Fielding Smith* (Salt Lake City: The Church of Jesus Christ of Latter-day Saints, 2013).

of miracles including raising William D. Huntington from the dead (see Levi Curtis, *Juvenile Instructor*, 27:385–86). He saw God and was visited by angels. He uttered over one hundred prophecies which have been literally fulfilled, including prophesying the Civil War twenty-nine years before it began and the very state, South Carolina, where it would commence. Finally, he sealed his testimony with his own blood. He died a martyr for the cause of Christ."

They looked at us with astonishment. We smiled at them with joy and humble gratitude for our membership in the "true and living church" of Jesus Christ.

6

Are Mormons Christian?

I was invited to speak at a missionary fireside in Garden Grove, California. My assigned topic was "Are Mormons Christian?" For fifty minutes I explained, rapid-fire style, that "the Lord's directive for the name of His Church [is] The Church of Jesus Christ of Latter-day Saints." (See 3 Nephi 27:1–9 and D&C 115:3–4.) Elder James E. Talmage taught, "There are churches named after their place of origin—as the Church of England; other sects are designated in honor of their famous promoters—as Lutherans, Calvinists, Wesleyans; others are known from some peculiarity of creed or doctrine—as Methodists, Presbyterians, and Baptists; but down to the beginning of the nineteenth century there was no church even claiming name or title as the Church of Christ."[20]

I shared that Latter-day Saints obey the commandment, "Whatsoever ye shall do, ye shall do it in my name" (3 Nephi 27:7).

Every ordinance performed is done in His name. Every prayer, baptism, conformation, blessing, ordination, sermon, testimony, lesson and marriage is concluded with the invocation of His sacred name. It is in His name that the sick are healed, and other miracles are performed.

In the sacrament, we take upon ourselves the name of Jesus Christ. We covenant to always remember Him and keep His commandments. He is central in all that we believe.

Elder Boyd K. Packer taught,

> Christ's presence is found also in the standard works of the Church—Bible, Book of Mormon, Doctrine and Covenants, and Pearl of Great Price. In the Topical Guide are eighteen pages, very fine print, single-spaced references to the subject of Jesus Christ, which is the most comprehensive compilation of scriptural references on the subject of the Lord Jesus Christ that has ever been assembled in the history of the world.

20. James E. Talmage, *The Great Apostasy*, 158.

Christ dominates the Book of Mormon, page by page, being referred to in 3,925 verses—more than half of its 6,607 verses.[21]

I informed them, "He is known by 101 titles in the Book of Mormon. Whether descriptively designated as Only Begotten Son, Creator, Advocate, Mediator, Prince of Peace, Son of God, Messiah, Savior, Author and Finisher of Salvation, or King of Kings, the Book of Mormon testifies more often and more powerfully that Jesus is the Christ than any other book ever written, 25 percent more than even the New Testament. This is why the Prophet Joseph Smith testified, 'I told the brethren that the Book of Mormon was the most correct of any book on earth and the keystone of our religion, and a man would get nearer to God by abiding by its precepts, than by any other book'" (introduction to the Book of Mormon).

I shared, "The hymns we sing are praises unto the Lord: 'I Believe in Christ,' 'I Know That My Redeemer Lives,' 'Upon the Cross of Calvary,' 'The Lord is My Light,' etc."

The stake president had informed the audience that after my remarks we would assemble in the cultural hall for refreshments and I would answer their questions.

Six men from Calvary Chapel learned of the fireside on the internet. They were the first to approach me. They said, "You are not Christian."

I inquired, "What part of my talk did you not understand?"

They rephrased their statement, "You worship another Jesus."

I then asked them, "Did Jesus have a God?"

They answered, "No, Jesus is God!"

I followed with, "Did Jesus have a Father?"

They responded, "Jesus is the Father and the Son!"

I had them read Ephesians 1:3: "Blessed be the God and Father of our Lord Jesus Christ." I told them, "According to Paul, Jesus had a God and Father." I then directed them to John 14:28: "I go unto the Father: for my Father is greater than I." Then I asked, "What does this verse teach us about the Father of Jesus?"

They replied, "The Father is greater than Jesus."

---

21. Boyd K. Packer, "Be 'Peaceable Followers of Christ,'" *Church News*, 7 February 1998, 3.

The third scripture I shared was John 20:17 when the risen Christ appeared to Mary Magdalene. "Jesus saith unto her, Touch me not; for I am not yet ascended to my Father: but go to my brethren, and say unto them, I ascend unto my Father, and your Father; and to my God, and your God." I testified, "Jesus not only had a God and Father but the God and Father of Jesus is my God and Father and your God and Father." *The truth of the matter is that it's in everybody's Bible!*

I explained further, "We worship Jesus the Christ, the son of the living God (Matthew 16:16) as found in the New Testament. We do not worship the Jesus of the Nicene Creed. We are biblical, not 'credo' Christians! These creeds are post-biblical and non-biblical."

They had no further questions.

7

What is the role of women in your church?

I participated on a panel with other religious leaders. We were asked, "What is the role of women in your church?"

The Jewish rabbi was very quiet. The Muslim had nothing to contribute. The Catholic priest said, "Our nuns dedicate their lives to the Lord's service."

The Evangelical minister proudly proclaimed, "Women can be ministers in our church!"

When it was my turn, I testified into the microphone, "The role of a woman in The Church of Jesus Christ of Latter-day Saints is to become a queen of heaven!" The rabbi leaned so far forward to look at me that he almost fell out of his chair. To elaborate on my answer, I paraphrased Elder Bruce R. McConkie: "God is our Eternal Father; we also have an Eternal Mother. There is no such thing as a father without a mother, nor can there be children without parents."[22]

Elder Dallin H. Oaks explained, "Our theology begins with heavenly parents. Our highest aspiration is to be like them."[23]

Quoting Glenn L. Pace, I testified, "When you stand in front of your heavenly parents in those royal courts on high and you look into Her eyes and behold Her countenance, any question you ever had about . . . [the nature of the Godhead and Heavenly Mother] will evaporate into the rich celestial air, because at that moment you will see standing directly in front of you, your divine nature and destiny."[24]

I reiterated, "What greater blessing could any woman receive? The Lord's Church exalts women!"

---

22. See Bruce R. McConkie, "Mother in Heaven," *Mormon Doctrine,* 516–17.
23. Dallin H. Oaks, *LDS Living*, Oct. 23, 2015.
24. Glenn L. Pace, "The Divine Nature and Destiny of Women," Devotional Address, BYU, Provo, Utah, March 9, 2010.

8

What is your position on same-sex marriage?

The honor students at Aliso Niguel High School (California) were asked, "What can we do to honor you?" They wanted a religious panel where they could ask the various church spokespeople anything they wanted. I was invited to represent our church.

Because we had no idea what their questions would be, I tried to anticipate some important topics. For example, because of the recent Supreme Court decision, I fully expected them to ask us about same-sex marriage, so I memorized the First Presidency's letter on the subject. Sure enough, question number three was, "What is your position on same-sex marriage?"

I thought the rabbi would read the words of Moses on the subject in the Torah. However, he evaded the question. The Muslim did not respond and passed the microphone. I supposed the Evangelical minister would share the Apostle Paul's epistle to the Romans, but he simply replied, "Anyone and everyone can come to my church regardless of their sexual orientation."

I was next and explained, "A chief attribute of a true Christian is that we love one another (see John 13:34–35). Members of the Church of Jesus Christ love all of God's children as our brothers and sisters."

I continued by reciting, "Changes in the civil law do not—indeed cannot—change the moral law that God has established. God expects us to uphold and keep His commandments regardless of divergent opinions or trends in society. His law of chastity is clear: sexual relations are proper only between a man and a woman who are legally and lawfully wedded as husband and wife."[25]

"Former US President Jimmy Carter wisely stated, 'We must adjust to changing times and still hold to unchanging principles.'"[26]

---

25. First Presidency letter, March 6, 2014.
26. President of the United States Jimmy Carter Inaugural Address January 20, 1977.

I had time remaining in my two-minute allotment to quote President Gordon B. Hinckley: "Our opposition to attempts to legalize same-sex marriage should never be interpreted as justification for hatred, intolerance, or abuse of those who profess homosexual tendencies. . . . We love and honor them as sons and daughters of God. They are welcome in the Church. It is expected, however, that they follow the same God-given rules of conduct that apply to everyone else, whether single or married."[27]

The students in the auditorium were stunned. There was complete silence. It was as if the air went out of the room.

Before answering the next question, the Hindu said, "May I make a comment before you start the timer?" The moderator agreed. He put his arm around me and said, "Mr. Greiner knew his answer would not be received well by this audience. He is the only one of us who is quoting scripture and who memorizes the official position of his church on every topic we discuss. I find it refreshing to see someone stand up for what they believe regardless of public sentiment."

The audience broke into applause even though they were told to refrain from clapping until the event concluded.

> Dare to be a Mormon;
> Dare to stand alone.
> Dare to have a purpose firm;
> Dare to make it known.[28]

---

27. Gordon B. Hinckley, in Conference Report, Oct. 1999, 70.
28. Thomas S. Monson, "Dare to Stand Alone," *Ensign*, Nov. 2011.

9

You cannot destroy the truth
by refusing to accept it

Dianne and I had enough extra points on our credit card to enjoy a free weekend at the Marriott Hotel in Salt Lake City. I was wearing a BYU T-shirt when we went to the swimming pool. A tourist from Florida asked if I was a Mormon. It was obvious because the letters on my shirt were six inches tall. I was a walking billboard for Brigham Young University. He immediately began aggressively attacking the Church. I had compassion on this man because BYU had just defeated Miami in football. They were the defending national champions and the pre-season number-one ranked team.

I was on vacation and wanted to relax and enjoy my time with my wife, but this man's vicious remarks couldn't be ignored. Besides, there were about six or eight others listening to our conversation in the jacuzzi. After hearing his tirade without interrupting, I asked if I could share with him two quotes and two scriptures. He agreed.

I offered a silent prayer and felt impressed to say, "Now talk about this kingdom being destroyed! . . . Why, you might as well try to pluck the stars from the firmament or the moon or the sun from its orbit! It can never be accomplished, for it is the work of the Almighty. I advise every man who has a disposition to put forth his hand against this work, to hold on and consider. Take the advice of Gamaliel the lawyer. Said he: 'If this is the work of God, ye can do nothing against it; if it is not, it will come to naught.'"[29] I explained, "You cannot destroy the truth by refusing to accept it."

For my second scripture and quote, I shared 1 Peter 2:15, which reads, "For so is the will of God, that with well doing ye may put to silence the ignorance of foolish men."

This angry gentleman inquired of me, "Are you calling me a fool?"

---

29. Lorenzo Snow, *Journal of Discourses*, 14:307.

I smiled and said kindly, "Never ever would I call you a fool, sir. Peter did, but not I." I continued and explained that Joseph Smith was asked, "What is required to constitute good church membership?"

In response to the question Joseph Smith said, among other things, "He is to feed the hungry, to clothe the naked, to provide for the widow, to dry up the tear of the orphan, to comfort the afflicted, whether in this church, or in any other, or in no church at all, wherever he finds them."[30]

I said to my antagonist, "Whenever there is a fire, flood, earthquake, tornado, hurricane, or natural disaster, members of The Church of Jesus Christ of Latter-day Saints are the first ones on the scene offering relief to those in need all over the world both in and out of our Church. 'True Christianity is love in action.'[31] As you come to know us better you will see Christians in word and deed that strive to go about doing good."

This must have taken the wind out of his sails because his mean-spirited mud throwing was replaced with complimentary comments about our members.

---

30. Joseph Smith, *Times and Seasons*, 15 March 1842, 732.
31. David O. McKay, quoted in *Favorite Quotations from the Collection of Thomas S. Monson*, 44.

10

Why isn't the Book of Mormon mentioned in the Bible?

I've been asked on numerous occasions, "If the Book of Mormon is the word of God, why isn't it mentioned in the Bible?

Oliver Cowdery declared: "I wrote with my own pen the entire Book of Mormon (save a few pages) as it fell from the lips of the Prophet Joseph Smith, as he translated it by the gift and power of God. . . . It contains the everlasting Gospel, and came forth to the children of men **in fulfillment of the revelations**. . . . I beheld with my eyes, and handled with my hands, the gold plates from which it was translated."[32]

The following are prophecies of the Book of Mormon recorded in the Bible.

Revelation 14:6

> And I saw another angel fly in the midst of heaven, having the everlasting gospel to preach unto them that dwell on the earth, and to every nation, and kindred, and tongue, and people.

President N. Eldon Tanner confirmed, "This revelation was fulfilled . . . when the Angel Moroni . . . appeared to Joseph Smith and told him of the plates which contained the gospel in its fullness. Joseph said that as the Angel Moroni appeared to him, he called him by name and told him that 'there was a book deposited written upon gold plates, giving an account of the former inhabitants of this continent, and the source from whence they sprang.' He also said that the fulness of the everlasting gospel was contained in it, as delivered by the Savior to the ancient inhabitants."[33]

---

32. "Last Days of Oliver Cowdery," *Deseret News*, Apr. 13, 1859, 48.
33. N. Eldon Tanner, in Conference Report, April 1964, 62. See also Joseph Smith—History 1:33–34.

From this prophecy I know why the Angel Moroni is atop many of our temples. But I wondered why he had a trumpet to his lips until I read this article in the January 2000 *Ensign* article "Feast of Trumpets":

> On 22 September 1827, the very day Israel celebrated the Feast of Trumpets, Moroni gave the golden plates to the Prophet Joseph Smith.
>
> . . . [The] Feast of Trumpets . . . signifies
>
> (1) the beginning of Israel's final harvest,
>
> (2) the day God had set to remember His ancient promises to regather Israel,
>
> (3) a time for new revelation that would lead to a new covenant with Israel, and
>
> (4) a time to prepare for the Millennium.
>
> The Hebrew name used today for the Feast of Trumpets is Rosh Hashanah, which is the Jewish New Year. But this was not its original name, though the day does signify a new beginning.
>
> One of its original names was the Day of Remembrance. This name arose because the Lord commanded Israel to blow trumpets on this day for remembrance.
>
> . . . It was on this day that the Israelites were remembered and freed from slavery in Egypt . . .
>
> The blowing of the trumpet is the major ritual of the Feast of Trumpets. Because the first mention of the trumpet is at Mount Sinai, these instruments are seen by Jewish writers as a symbol of revelation . . . .The day's services also include petitions to God to rebuild His temple—the place where covenants are made—as He promised. The sound of the trumpets, which occurred in this religious service in 1827, did indeed precede new revelation that has led to the making of new covenants in new temples with an Israel now being regathered. . . The golden plates were delivered to the young Prophet Joseph Smith early in the morning of 22 September 1827. The Feast of Trumpets, with prayers pleading for God's remembrance of his still-exiled people, had begun at sundown the previous evening. The services continued that morning, with a worldwide sounding of the ram's horn.
>
> Unbeknown to Judah, all that those horns represented was now to be fulfilled. For on this day, God remembered His people and set in motion His plan to regather them.

On that day, God's final harvest began. On that day, new revelation was granted which would bring a return to renewed covenants. From that day onward, Israel would be called to repentance in preparation for Christ's return and reign. The Book of Mormon exists to serve these ends. Today, Moroni's image trumpets from temple spires around the world a final call to awaken, repent, and prepare.[34]

Isaiah 29:17–19, 24

Is it not yet a very little while, and Lebanon shall be turned into a fruitful field, and the fruitful field shall be esteemed as a forest?

And in that day shall the deaf hear the words of the book, and the eyes of the blind shall see out of obscurity, and out of darkness.

The meek also shall increase their joy in the Lord, and the poor among men shall rejoice in the Holy One of Israel.

They also that erred in spirit shall come to understanding, and they that murmured shall learn doctrine.

Elder Mark E. Peterson said:

Isaiah indicated that Palestine, long languishing in the grip of the desert, was destined to be turned, into a fruitful field in connection with the gathering of the Jews to their homeland. . . .

A sacred book was to come forth before that time. . . .

. . . Where is that book?

It is one of the signs of the times . . . Isaiah set a limit on the time of its publication. That time limit was related to the period when fertility would return to Palestine. Isaiah said that the book would come forth first, and then added that in "a very little while . . . Lebanon shall be turned into a fruitful field, and the fruitful field shall be esteemed as a forest" [Isaiah 29:17] The time limit was expired. This new volume of scripture must have come forth before now or Isaiah was not a true prophet, for Palestine is fruitful again.[35]

---

34. Lenet Hadley Read, *Ensign*, January 2000, 25–29.
35. Mark E. Peterson, in Conference Report, Oct. 1965, 61.

Isaiah 29:11–12

And the vision of all is become unto you as the words of a book that is sealed which men deliver to one that is learned, saying, Read this, I pray thee: and he saith, I cannot; for it is sealed: And the book is delivered to him that is not learned, saying, Read this, I pray thee: and he saith, I am not learned.

From Joseph Smith's history we learn:

I [Martin Harris] went to the city of New York, and presented the characters which had been translated, with the translation thereof, to Professor Charles Anthon, a gentleman celebrated for his literary attainments. Professor Anthon stated that the translation was correct, more so than any he had before seen translated from the Egyptian. I then showed him those which were not yet translated, and he said that they were Egyptian, Chaldaic, Assyriac, and Arabic; and he said they were true characters. He gave me a certificate, certifying to the people of Palmyra that they were true characters, and that the translation of such of them as had been translated was also correct. I took the certificate and put it into my pocket, and was just leaving the house, when Mr. Anthon called me back, and asked me how the young man found out that there were gold plates in the place where he found them. I answered that an angel of God had revealed it unto him.

He then said to me, "Let me see that certificate." I accordingly took it out of my pocket and gave it to him, when he took it and tore it to pieces, saying that there was no such thing now as ministering of angels and that if I would bring the plates to him he would translate them. I informed him that part of the plates were sealed and that I was forbidden to bring them. He replied, "I cannot read a sealed book." I left him and went to Dr. Mitchell, who sanctioned what Professor Anthon had said respecting both the characters and the translation. (Joseph Smith—History 1:64–65)

To further illustrate that Joseph Smith was the unlearned man spoken of by Isaiah, Joseph's wife Emma wrote the following:

Joseph Smith (as a young man) . . . could neither write nor dictate a coherent and well-worded letter, let alone dictate a book like the Book of Mormon, and though I was an active participant in the scenes that transpired, was present during the translation of the plates, and had cognizance of things as they transpired, it is marvelous to me—a marvel and a wonder—as much as to anyone else . . . . My belief is that the Book of Mormon is of divine authenticity—I have not the slightest doubt of it. . . . when acting as his scribe, your father (she was being interrogated by her son) would dictate to me hour after hour; and when returning after meals, or interruptions, he would at once begin where he had left off, without either seeing the manuscript or having any portion of it read to him. This was an unusual thing for him to do. It would have been improbable that a learned man could do this and for one so ignorant and unlearned as he was, it was simply impossible."[36]

Isaiah 29:4

And thou shalt be brought down, and shalt speak out of the ground, and thy speech shall be low out of the dust, and thy voice shall be, as of one that hath a familiar spirit, out of the ground, and thy speech shall whisper out of the dust.

From Joseph Smith's own account we learn the following:

Convenient to the village of Manchester, Ontario county, New York, stands a hill of considerable size, and the most elevated of any in the neighborhood. On the west side of this hill, not far from the top, under a stone of considerable size, lay the plates, deposited in a stone box. This stone was thick and rounding in the middle on the upper side, and thinner towards the edges, so that the middle part of it was visible above the ground, but the edge all around was covered with earth.

Having removed the earth, I obtained a lever, which I got fixed under the edge of the stone, and with a little exertion raised it up. I looked in, and there indeed did I behold the plates, the Urim and Thummim, and the breastplate, as stated by the messenger. The box in which they lay was formed by laying stones together in some kind of cement. In the bottom of the box were laid two stones crossways of the box, and on these stones lay the plates and the other things with them. (Joseph Smith—History 1:51–52)

---

36. Emma Smith, *The Witnesses of the Book of Mormon*, compiled by Preston Nibley, 28–29.

Out of the Ground:

Never was a prophecy more truly fulfilled than this, in the coming forth of the Book of Mormon. Joseph Smith took that sacred history 'out of the ground.' It is the voice of the ancient prophets of America speaking 'out of the ground;' their speech is 'low out of the dust;' it speaks in a most familiar manner of the doings of bygone ages; it is the voice of those who slumber in the dust. It is the voice of prophets speaking from the dead, crying repentance in the ears of the living. In what manner could a nation, after they were brought down and destroyed, 'speak out of the ground?' . . . Their voice, speech or words, can only 'speak out of the ground,' or 'whisper out of the dust' by their books or writings being discovered.[37]

Isaiah 29:13–14

Wherefore the Lord said, Forasmuch as this people draw near me with their mouth, and with their lips do honor me, but have removed their heart far from me, and their fear toward me is taught by the precept of men:

Therefore, behold, I will proceed to do a marvelous work among this people, even a marvelous work and a wonder: for the wisdom of their wise men shall perish, and the understanding of their prudent men shall be hid.

In an *Ensign* article, Elder Neal A. Maxwell wrote the following: "Some things we know about the process of translation further qualify the Book of Mormon as a *'marvelous work & wonder'*. One marvel is the very rapidity with which Joseph was translating. The total translation time was about 65 working days. By comparison, more than 50 [eminent] English scholars labored for seven years, using previous translations, to produce the King James Version of the Bible."[38]

Just as fingerprints identify people one from another, word-prints identify authors from each other:

---

37. Orson Pratt, *Orson Pratt's Works: The Light of Understanding*, Vol. 1 (Salt Lake City, Deseret News Press, 1945), 271.See also Psalm 85:11; Moses 7:62.
38. Neal A. Maxwell, *Ensign*, January 1997, 39.

Two statisticians, Dr. Alvin C. Rencher of BYU and Dr. Wayne A. Larsen of the Eyring Research Center, employed newly developed computer techniques to identify "word-prints" of different authors in the Book of Mormon. Their findings should permanently lay to rest the theories that Joseph Smith, Solomon Spaulding, or any other person associated with the Church around the time of the publication of the Book of Mormon authored the work. In the Book of Mormon study, Doctors Rencher and Larsen analyzed more than two hundred 1,000-word passages using three different word-prints and then verified the results using three separate statistical methods. "No matter the word-print or method used, the results indicated the same: the Book of Mormon is the work of many authors. The statisticians identified and developed reliable word-prints for 24 separate authors. It was also found that the word-prints of contemporary writers (Joseph Smith, Sidney Rigdon, Solomon Spaulding, William W. Phelps, Oliver Cowdery, and Parley P. Pratt) differ from those of the Book of Mormon writers. Statistically, say the researchers, the odds against a single author for the Book of Mormon exceed 100 billion to one.[39]

The Book of Mormon is truly a marvelous work and a wonder!

Ezekiel 37:15–17

The word of the Lord came again unto me, saying,
Moreover, thou son of man, take thee one stick, and write upon it, For Judah, and for the children of Israel his companions: then take another stick, and write upon it, For Joseph, the stick of Ephraim, and for all the house of Israel his companions: And join them one to another into one stick; and they shall become one in thine hand.

The Bible is "the stick of Judah," a record of the Jews. Jesus Christ is from the tribe of Judah. But what qualifies the Book of Mormon as the stick of Joseph"? After Nephi obtains the brass plates from Laban, his father, Lehi, searches his family history and learns he is from the

---

39. Marc Haddock, *Brigham Young University Today*, Nov. 1979, Vol. 133, No. 7.

tribe of Joseph of the twelve tribes of Israel. The Book of Mormon is a record of Lehi's posterity in the Americas.

1 Nephi 5:14

> And it came to pass that my father, Lehi, also found upon the plates of brass a genealogy of his fathers; wherefore he knew he knew that he was a descendant of Joseph . . .

Elder Body K. Packer explained, "In ancient Israel records were written upon tablets of wood or scrolls rolled upon sticks. The stick or record of Judah--the Old Testament and the New Testament--and the stick or record of Joseph--the Book of Mormon, which is another testament of Jesus Christ—are . . . indeed one in our hands. Ezekiel's prophecy now stands fulfilled."[40]

John 10:14–16

> I am the good shepherd and know my sheep, and am known of mine.
> As the Father knoweth me, even so know I the Father: and I lay down my life for the sheep.
> And other sheep I have, which are not of this fold: them also I must bring, and they shall hear my voice; and there shall be one fold and one shepherd.

President Joseph Fielding Smith made clear, "It is thought by some that [Christ] had reference to the Gentiles, but he said himself that he was not sent to the Gentiles, but to the lost sheep of the house of Israel (Matthew 15:24). He must have had reference to Israelites who were not in Palestine, and the visitation must have been one after His resurrection. There is no reference to such a visit in any of the four gospels, and the remark was made shortly before His death. When the Savior visited the Nephites He told them plainly that this reference to other sheep was a reference to them."[41]

---

40. Boyd K. Packer, "Scriptures," *Ensign*, November 1982, 51.
41. See 3 Nephi 15:21; Joseph Fielding Smith, *Doctrines of Salvation*, 214.

The crowning event of the Book of Mormon is the account of the Savior's visit to the Americas after His resurrection found in 3 Nephi 11:7–15:

> Behold my Beloved Son, in whom I am well pleased, in whom I have glorified my name—hear ye him.
>
> And it came to pass, as they understood they cast their eyes up again towards heaven; and behold, they saw a Man descending out of heaven; and he was clothed in a white robe; and he came down and stood in the midst of them . . .
>
> And it came to pass that he stretched forth his hand and spake unto the people saying:
>
> Behold, I am Jesus Christ, whom the prophets testified shall come into the world.
>
> And behold, I am the light and the life of the world; and I have drunk out of that bitter cup which the Father hath given me, and have glorified the Father in taking upon me the sins of the world, in the which I have suffered the will of the Father in all things from the beginning.
>
> And it came to pass that when Jesus had spoken these words the whole multitude fell to the earth; for they remembered that it had been prophesied among them that Christ should show himself unto them after his ascension into heaven.
>
> And it came to pass that the Lord spake unto them saying:
>
> Arise and come forth unto me, that ye may thrust your hands into my side, and also that ye may feel the prints of the nails in my hands and in my feet, that ye may know that I am the God of Israel, and the God of the whole earth, and have been slain for the sins of the world.
>
> And it came to pass that the multitude went forth, and thrust their hands into his side, and did feel the prints of the nails in his hands and in his feet; and this they did do, going forth one by one until they had all gone forth, and did see with their eyes and did feel with their hands, and did know of a surety and did bear record, that it was he, of whom it was written by the prophets, that should come.

The truth of the matter is that these prophecies have been fulfilled and are in everybody's Bible!

I like to share a parable by Hugh Nibley with my friends not of our faith who dismiss the Book of Mormon without reading it and applying Moroni's promise (see Moroni 10:4–5):

> A young man once long ago claimed he had found a large diamond in his field as he was plowing. He put the stone on display to the public free of charge, and everyone took sides. A psychologist showed, by citing some famous case studies, that the young man was suffering from a well-known form of delusion. An historian showed that other men have also claimed to have found diamonds in fields and have been deceived. A geologist proved that there were no diamonds in the area but only quartz: The young man had been fooled by a quartz. When asked to inspect the stone itself, the geologist declined with a weary, tolerant smile, and a kindly shake of the head. An English professor showed that the young man in describing his stone used the very same language that others had used in describing uncut diamonds: He was, therefore, simply speaking the common language of his time. A sociologist showed that only three out of 177 florists' assistants in four major cities believed the stone was genuine. A clergyman wrote a book to show that it was not the young man but someone else who had found the stone. Finally an indignant jeweler . . . pointed out that since the stone was still available for examination the answer to the question of whether it was a diamond or not had absolutely nothing to do with who found it or whether the finder was honest or sane, or who believed him, or whether he would know a diamond from a brick, or whether diamonds had ever been found in fields, or whether people had ever been fooled by quartz or glass but was to be answered simply and solely by putting the stone to certain well-known tests for diamonds. Experts on diamonds were called in. Some of them declared it genuine. The others made nervous jokes about it and declared that they could not very well jeopardize their dignity and reputations by appearing to take the thing too seriously. To hide the bad impression thus made, someone came out with the theory that the stone was really a synthetic diamond, very skillfully made, but a fake just the same. The objection to this is that the production of a good synthetic diamond, for the farm boy, would have been an even more remarkable feat than the finding of a real one.[42]

---

42. Hugh Nibley, *Lehi in the Desert and the World of the Jaredites* (Salt Lake City: Bookcraft, 1952), 136–137.

11

Isn't 1 Corinthians 15:29 about baptism for the dead simply a rhetorical question?

The Bible is inerrant! How do you justify your eighth article of faith?

Shortly after the dedication of the Newport Beach California Temple, I was invited to address eighty students from Calvary Baptist High School and answer their questions. Because we were on the sacred temple grounds, I thought they would be reverent and respectful. To my surprise they each asked an anti-Mormon question. Over the years I have heard just about all of these tired, worn-out, recycled questions, but there were two that may be of interest to share.

My first name is Russell. Two of our Apostles have the name Russell. I have never met a Russell I didn't like, but the students' junior pastor (also named Russell) may have been the first. When I explained baptism for the dead and quoted "Else what shall they do which are baptized for the dead, if the dead rise not at all? Why are they then baptized for the dead? (1 Corinthians 15:29)," Reverend Russ said, "First Corinthians 15:29 is simply a rhetorical question."

When I speak to groups not of our faith, I bring a notebook containing all my mission prep handouts. They really came in handy. My answer stunned him and his students. I explained, "The New English Bible renders the verse: 'Again, there are those who receive baptism on behalf of the dead. Why should they do this? If the dead are not raised to life at all, what do they mean by being baptized on their behalf?'

"The Council of Carthage, held in 397 A.D., clearly declares that the Christians of that date did practice vicarious baptisms for the dead, for in the sixth cannon of that council the prevailing church forbids any further administration of baptism for the dead. Why should this cannon be formed against this practice if it had no existence among the Christians of those days?"[43]

---

43. Mark E. Petersen, *Utah Genealogical and Historical Magazine*, April 1933, 63.

Non-LDS scholars commented on the ordinance of baptism for the dead: "The apostle is writing about persons who are physically dead. It appears that under the pressure of concern for the eternal destiny of dead relatives or friends some people in the church were undergoing baptism on their behalf in the belief that this would enable the dead to receive the benefits of Christ's salvation."[44]

As evidence of the longevity of the practice of baptism for the dead, the fifth century Father Epiphanius reported the following regarding a sect of Christians known as the Marcionites: "From Asia and Gaul has reached us the account of a certain practice, namely that when any die without baptism among them, they baptize others in their place and in their name, so that, rising in the resurrection, they will not have to pay the penalty of having failed to receive baptism . . . For this reason this tradition which has reached us is said to be the very thing to which the Apostle himself refers [in 1 Corinthians 15:29]."[45]

The other question by Reverend Russ had nothing to do with the temple. He declared before his students, "How do you justify your eighth article of faith: 'We believe the Bible to be the word of God as far as it is translated correctly'?" The reverend declared emphatically, "The Bible is inerrant and infallible!"

I responded, "The Prophet Joseph Smith said, 'I believe the Bible as it read when it came from the pen of the original writers. Ignorant translators, careless transcribers, or designing and corrupt priests have committed many errors.'"[46] I continued, "We do not have the original manuscripts of any of the books of the New Testament but only copies. These copies are centuries removed from the originals. All of these copies contain mistakes, as scribes either inadvertently or intentionally altered the text."[47]

---

44. William F. Orr and James Arthur Walther, *The Anchor Bible: 1 Corinthians* (New York: Doubleday, 1976), 337.
45. Epiphanius, "Against Heresies," 1:28 & 6, cited in Hugh Nibley, *Mormonism and Early Christianity* (Provo, UT: FARMS, 1987), 12–126.
46. Joseph Fielding Smith, *Teachings of the Prophet Joseph Smith*, 327.
47. Bart D. Ehrman, *Misquoting Jesus*, 260.

The Johannine Comma in 1 John 5:7 states: "For there are three that bear record in heaven, the Father, the word, and the Holy Ghost: and these three are one."

Nearly all recent translations of the Bible have removed this clause, as it does not appear in older copies of the epistle before the sixteenth century, nor was it quoted by any of the early church fathers in their Trinitarian debates. Bart D. Ehrman, in his book *Misquoting Jesus: The Story Behind Who Changed The Bible And Why*, explains how the Johannine Comma "cannot be found in the oldest and superior manuscripts of the Greek New Testament."

Other contradictions in the Bible include:

Acts 9:7: The men journeying with Paul heard a voice, but saw no man.

Acts 22:9: They saw the light, but they heard not the voice that spake to me.

2 Samuel 24:1–2: The Lord moved David to take a census

1 Chronicles 21:1–2: Satan provoked David to take the census

2 Kings 8:26: Ahaziah began his reign at age 22.

2 Chronicles 22:2: He began at age 42

Matthew 27:5: Judas died by hanging himself

Acts 1:18: He fell, burst open, and his bowels gushed out

Matthew 1:16: Jacob was Joseph's father

Luke 3:23: Heli was Joseph's father

Mark 15:25: Jesus was crucified the third hour

John 19:14: He was still before Pilot the sixth hour

2 Kings 16:5: Ahaz was conquered

2 Chronicles 28:5: Ahaz was not conquered

1 Corinthians 15:5: Resurrected Christ seen by the twelve apostles

Matthew 27:3–5: Judas hanged himself before the resurrection

Again, I testified that "the Bible is the word of God as far as it is translated correctly."

12

The prophet Isaiah taught, "Before me there was no God." Therefore, Mormon doctrine that man can become a god must be false!

The prophet Isaiah taught, "Before me there was no God formed, neither shall there be after me" (Isaiah 43:10). Some have challenged, "You believe that the Bible is the word of God; that Isaiah was a prophet of God; that Jesus quoted Isaiah in his mortal ministry more than any other prophet; and that Jesus says in your Book of Mormon, 'A commandment I give unto you that ye search these things diligently; for great are the words of Isaiah' (3 Nephi 23:1). Therefore, Mormon doctrine that man can become a god must be false" (see also Isaiah 44:8; 45:5; 46:9).

The context of these verses is that God was reprimanding the Israelites because they were worshipping graven images and statues made with man's hands. On repeated occasions the Lord declared in these chapters that none of these images or statues, whether formed in the past or in the future, would ever be a god. These verses had everything to do with the incapacity of graven images to become gods and absolutely nothing to do with man's capacity to become a god. The headnotes for Isaiah 46 reads, "Idols are not to be compared with the Lord-He alone is God and shall save Israel."

Isaiah 46:5–7 clarifies this explanation perfectly: "To whom will ye liken me, and make me equal, and compare me, that we may be like? They lavish gold out of the bag, and weigh silver in the balance, and hire a goldsmith: and he maketh it a god: they fall down, yea, they worship. They bear him upon the shoulder, they carry him, and set him in his place, and he standeth; from his place shall he not remove: yea, one shall cry unto him, yet can he not answer, nor save him out of his trouble."

13

"Ye shall know them by their fruits"

I enjoyed a memorable one-on-one visit with a Presbyterian minister. His father-in-law joined the Church and moved to Utah. During family gatherings, they discuss religion and have strong doctrinal disagreements. Because I am a convert from the Presbyterian faith, the minister requested we meet to answer his questions so he could better understand our beliefs.

I explained to him that from the beginning God revealed and administered the gospel through prophets. He asked, "How would you define a prophet?"

I recited Deuteronomy 18:18: "I will raise them up a prophet from among their brethren, like unto thee, and will put my words in his mouth; and he shall speak unto them all that I shall command him."

I then related Joseph Smith's First Vision: "I saw a pillar of light exactly over my head, above the brightness of the sun, which descended gradually until it fell upon me. When the light rested upon me I saw two Personages, whose brightness and glory defy all description, standing above me in the air. One of them spake unto me, calling me by name and said, pointing to the other—*This is My Beloved Son. Hear Him!*" (Joseph Smith—History 1:16–17).

I followed up by quoting Numbers 12:6–8: "And he said, Hear now my words: If there be a prophet among you, I the Lord will make myself known unto him in a vision, and will speak unto him in a dream. My servant Moses is not so, who is faithful in all mine house. With him will I speak mouth to mouth . . . and the similitude of the Lord shall he behold." In addition to the still, small voice, the Lord communicates to His servants the prophets by visions, dreams, and in the case of major prophets like Moses and Joseph Smith, face to face.

I then testified that Joseph Smith had the same vision as did Stephen. "But he, being full of the Holy Ghost, looked up steadfastly into heaven, and saw the glory of God, and Jesus standing on the right hand of God, and said, Behold, I see the heavens opened, and the Son of man standing on the right hand of God" (Acts: 7:55–56).

I then quoted Joseph Fielding McConkie: "Joseph Smith . . . was . . . the first man since the writers of the Bible . . . to whom Christ personally appeared. . . . Adam, Enoch, Noah, Abraham, Moses, Elijah, John the Baptist, Peter, James, and John, among others from ancient times, all personally appeared to him and instructed him in the principles they taught during their mortal ministries.

". . . Each of these men laid their hands on his head and blessed him with the power and authority that was theirs during their mortal ministries. What theological school can match that kind of experience or training? The world can profess to know their Bible; Joseph Smith knew its authors. The world can profess to believe in Christ; Joseph Smith talked with Christ as one man talks with another."[48]

The minister asked, "Why do we need a prophet today when we have the Bible?"

I answered, quoting Elder Tad R. Callister, "God still speaks to man today. . . . The heavens are not closed. One need but ask three questions . . . to arrive at that conclusion. . . . First, does God love us as much today as He loved the people to whom He spoke in New Testament times? Second, does God have the same power today as He did then? And third, do we need Him as much today as they needed Him anciently? If the answers to those questions are yes and if God is the same yesterday, today and forever, as the scriptures so declare (see Hebrews 13:8), then there is little doubt: God does speak to man today exactly as Joseph Smith testified."[49]

Ralph Waldo Emerson said to the Divinity School at Harvard, "It is my duty to say to you that the need was never greater [for] new revelation than now. The doctrine of inspiration is lost. . . . Miracles, prophecy, . . . the holy life, exist as ancient history [only]. . . . Men have come to speak of . . . revelation as somewhat long ago given and

---

48. Joseph Fielding McConkie, "Joseph Smith and the One True Church Doctrine," *Meridian Magazine,* May 9, 2005.
49. Elder Tad R. Callister, *Ensign,* November 2009.

done, as if God were dead. . . . It is the office of a true teacher to show us that God is, not was; that He speaketh, not spake."[50]

I added, "It is an infallible sign of the true church that it has in it divinely chosen, living prophets to guide it, men who receive current revelation from God and whose recorded words become new scripture."[51]

We then read together the verses in the New Testament that explain the organization and offices in Christ's ancient church.

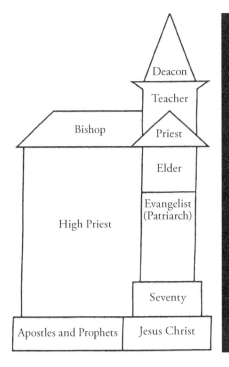

Eph. 2:19-21 Apostles & Prophets form the foundation.
Jesus Christ is the Chief Cornerstone. Building fitly framed. *Mark 3:14-18*
Eph. 4:11-14 **Apostles, Prophets, Evangelists (Patriarch), Pastors (Bishop) and Teachers.**
Luke 10:1 **Seventy**
Heb. 5:1, 10 **High Priest**
James 5:14-16 **Elders**
1 Tim. 3:1-7 **Bishop**
Luke 1 :8; Acts 6: 7 **Priest**
1 Tim. 3:8-10 **Deacon**

To illustrate that the Savior's restored church is identical to His former church, I shared this story by Elder LeGrand Richards:

> When we prepared the plans for the Los Angeles Temple and I was the Presiding Bishop, we showed those plans to the First Presidency. There were eighty-five pages, about four feet long and

50. *The Complete Essays and Other Writings of Ralph Waldo Emerson*, ed. Brooks Atkinson (1940), 75, 71, 80.
51. Mark E. Petersen, "Evidence of Things Not Seen," *Ensign*, May 1978, 61.

two and a half feet wide, and we did not have the plans for the electrical or the plumbing work. You could take those plans and you could go all over the world and try to fit them to any other building in the world, and you could not do it. There is only one building that they will fit, and that is the Los Angeles Temple. In that same sense, you can take the Bible and go all over this world, and you cannot fit it to any other church except [The Church of Jesus Christ of Latter-day Saints.][52]

We finished our discussion by reviewing Matthew 7:15–16: "Beware of false prophets, which come to you in sheep's clothing, but inwardly they are ravening wolves. Ye shall know them by their fruits. Do men gather grapes of thorns, or figs of thistles?"

I then related some of the fruits of the Church:

- The fastest growing church in the world. Four hundred churches a year are built, paid for, and dedicated just to keep up with the growth.
- The largest youth organization on earth (see Proverbs 22:6).
- The oldest and largest women's organization in the United States (see 1 Corinthians 13:8).
- More college graduates per capita than any other church or religion (see D&C 93:36; 130:18–19).
- The lowest mortality rate in the nation, living ten years longer than our peers (see Doctrine And Covenants 89).
- With the national divorce rate of over 50 percent, less than 6 percent of temple marriages end in divorce
- The highest birthrate. (He laughed when I told him, "Until the train traveled through Utah, the principle means of transportation was the baby carriage.")
- The state of Utah, which is 70 percent LDS, has the lowest crime rate in the country (see Articles of Faith 1:12).

What was the minister's reaction to all this? He admitted, "I feel like I am competing in a hockey game against a power play and I have no goalie!"

---

52. G. LaMont Richards, *LeGrand Richards Speaks*, 150.

14

Do you know how The Church of Jesus Christ of Latter-day Saints began?

Dianne and I serve as ordinance workers on Friday night in the Newport Beach California Temple. One evening as I walked out of the sealing room, a woman said to me, "You are Russ Greiner."

I responded, "I certainly am."

She added, "You spoke at our Relief Society birthday celebration in Ladera Ranch."

"Yes, I did." I asked, "May I share with you an experience I had that night with a woman not of our faith?"

She graciously agreed.

I explained, "After my talk, during dinner, three sisters came over to me and said, 'We brought a non-member friend tonight and she would love to talk with you.' I arose and followed them to her table.

"After introductions, the guest said to me, 'I attend Saddleback Church and Rick Warren has strong convictions. I listened to you tonight and can see that you have strong convictions. I'm conflicted!'

"I asked her, 'Do you know how Rick Warren began his church?'

"She confessed, 'I don't know.'

"I shared what Rick Warren has published: 'I began Saddleback Church by going door-to-door for twelve weeks and surveying the unchurched in my area. I wrote down in my notebook five questions I would use to start Saddleback:

"1. What do you think is the greatest need in this area?

"2. Are you actively attending any church?

"3. Why do you think most people don't attend church?

"4. If you were to look for a church to attend, what kind of things would you look for?

"5. What could I do for you?[53]

"I then asked her, 'Do you know how The Church of Jesus Christ of Latter-day Saints began?' She expressed, 'I have no idea.'

---

53. Rick Warren, *The Purpose Driven Church*, 244–245.

"I testified, 'God the Eternal Father and His Resurrected Son Jesus Christ appeared to Joseph Smith and called him to be a prophet through whom they restored the Church of Jesus Christ back on the earth!

"She replied, 'Wow!'"

As I completed telling this story to the sister in the temple, she informed me, "That woman joined the Church, Brother Greiner, and so did her husband and children."

Shortly thereafter I attended church in Ladera Ranch, California, for the missionary farewell of one of my mission prep all-stars. Before the sacrament service began, I felt a tap on my shoulder. As I turned around, there sat this very sister with her family.

15

It does make a difference which church you belong to

After class a seminary student told me of a discussion he had with his married sister. She is a born-again saved Christian. She argued, "It doesn't really matter which church we belong to. The important thing is that we accept Christ as our personal Savior."

My student Karl said, "I wanted to tell her the advantages of being a member of the Church, but I didn't know what to say."

I sat down at the piano and began to play "Chopsticks." I explained, "Some churches specialize in baptism by sprinkling, another claims God is Jehovah, another is unique by worshipping on Saturday. These churches are based on the philosophies of men mingled with their interpretation of the scriptures. Christ said, 'This people draweth nigh unto me with their mouth, and honoureth me with their lips; but their heart is far from me. But in vain they do worship me, teaching for doctrines the commandments of men'" (Matthew 15:8–9).

I asked Karl if he loved music. He replied in the affirmative. I inquired, "Would you be satisfied if you only had one octave to perform music?"

He answered, "No, obviously not!"

I then played a scale on the piano using the entire keyboard. I inquired, "What difference would it make if you could utilize all the piano keys?"

He answered, "I would not be restricted. I could play any type of music from rock and roll, jazz, church hymns, classical, country music, any and everything."

"To play beautiful music one would utilize all the keys not just a select few. The Church of Jesus Christ of Latter-day Saints embraces the fulness of the gospel." I asked, "Karl, would you be fulfilled belonging to a church that had only an octave of the truth?"

He replied, "Of course not."

I continued, "You have been baptized by immersion for the remission of sins by proper priesthood authority. The Lord revealed,

'Although a man should be baptized an hundred times it availeth him nothing, for you cannot enter in at the straight gate, . . . by your dead works' (D&C 22:2). The Lord does not accept ordinances performed without His authority. Baptism is a requirement to enter the celestial kingdom. Would you be willing to receive this ordinance without God's authority and approval, or would you rather be baptized by the priesthood so it is recorded in heaven?"

Karl replied, "I want the Lord to recognize my ordinances."

I said, "You hold the priesthood of God; the authority to act in His name to uplift others. Tell me, do you want to baptize your children, advance your sons through the priesthood, and bless your family in times of need? Or would you prefer to have a minister do this for you?"

Karl answered, "I want to be the patriarch of my family."

I questioned, "Someday, you and your future sweetheart will desire to be married. Do you want to be married 'till death do you part,' or for time and eternity in the temple?"

Karl replied, "Forever!"

I went on. "The Church of Jesus Christ of Latter-day Saints has additional scripture, a living prophet, and continuous revelation. During each dispensation, God revealed His word through his prophets. Would you be content knowing only what God revealed to Moses? Would you be satisfied having God's word through the time of Christ's apostles? Or would you desire to know 'all that God has revealed, all that he does now reveal, and what he will yet reveal?'" (see Articles of Faith 1:9).

Before I could continue, Karl interrupted, "Okay, why settle for only part of the gospel when you can enjoy the complete gospel?"

I bore my fervent testimony to Karl. "Point for point, organization for organization, teaching for teaching, ordinance for ordinance, fruit for fruit, and revelation for revelation, it only matches one church, The Church of Jesus Christ of Latter-day Saints. It does make a difference which church we belong to!"

16

Mormons believe they can work their way to heaven

Dianne and I were invited with an intimate group of twelve couples to witness a theological debate between former Dean of Religion at BYU Robert J. Millet and Reverend Lee Johnson, an evangelical minister.

One of the invited guests was the Reverend Robert A. Schuller of the Crystal Cathedral. His Sunday program, "The Hour of Power" is broadcast throughout the world. When I was introduced to Reverend Schuller, he asked me, "What do you do for a living, Russ?"

I informed him, "For ten years I taught in the seminary program where high school students get up early in the morning for an hour of scripture study before every school day, and over twenty years I have instructed at an Institute of Religion, which is affiliated with every college in America and at most universities throughout the world. This helps our youth and young adults put on the full armor of God every day to resist the fiery darts of the wicked."

He replied, "You Mormons do a lot of things right. My daughter is a good girl, but she wouldn't get up at 5:00 a.m. for a Bible study class before school, and I don't think many other kids would either." He then asked a second question, "I have an enormous payroll and overhead. How do you get the people in your church to serve without pay?"

I recited to him 1 Peter 5:2: "Feed the flock of God, which is among you, taking the oversight thereof, not by constraint, but willingly; not for filthy lucre, but of a ready mind." I informed him, "Love is the motive and Christ is the reason for the service we render in the Church. I have served as a bishop over six years, contributing about thirty hours of service each week and have never received a paycheck."

We then sat down in the family room to watch this debate. Because of the small size of the group, we were allowed to participate somewhat. My first comment came after the Reverend Lee Johnson said, "If I were pressed against the wall, I would have to say Mormons aren't Christians."

I raised my hand and informed Reverend Johnson that the Prophet Joseph Smith set forth the purpose of the Church when he declared, "It is the bringing of men and women to a knowledge of the eternal truth that Jesus is the Christ, the Redeemer and Savior of the world."[54] I asked the reverend if he had read the book *Mere Christianity* by C.S. Lewis.

He replied, "I have read it many times."

I directed him to Lewis's statement: "It is not for us to say who, in the deepest sense, is or is not close to the spirit of Christ. We do not see into men's hearts. We cannot judge, and are indeed forbidden to judge. It would be wicked arrogance for us to say that any man . . . is not a Christian."[55]

Reverend Johnson looked down and said, "I'm not familiar with that passage."

My second comment came later in the debate when Reverend Johnson said, "Mormons believe they can work their way to heaven."

I raised my hand and said, "That is not true."

He retorted, "Yes, it is."

I replied, "It is not your place to define our doctrine. The Book of Mormon clearly states our theology on this matter." I then recited 2 Nephi 2:8: "Wherefore, how great the importance to make these things known unto the inhabitants of the earth, that they may know that there is no flesh that can dwell in the presence of God, save it be through the merits, and mercy, and grace of the Holy Messiah" (see also 2 Nephi 10:23–24). I added, "He came to pay a debt he didn't owe because we owed a debt we couldn't pay."[56]

Reverend Johnson looked at me, paused a moment, and then changed the subject.

---

54. Quoted by President Thomas S. Monson in Conference Report, April 1995, 66.
55. *Mere Christianity* (New York: Touchstone, 1996), xi.
56. Gerrit W. Gong, "Hosanna and Hallelujah—The Living Christ: The Heart of Restoration and Easter," *Ensign*, May 2020, 52.

17

I'm an atheist—convince me!

The Mission Viejo Institute is a recognized student club at Saddleback College named the Latter-day Saint Student Association. Every Wednesday from 10:30 to noon I went down with the missionaries and members of the institute to invite students on campus to "come and see." I met a young man from the Ultimate Frisbee Club whose table was near ours. He said to me, "I'm an atheist."

About ten to twelve students gathered around supposing, "This'll be interesting to watch."

He inquired of me, "How can you get an atheist to believe? Convince me!"

I began by quoting Edwin Conklin, a Princeton University biologist, who said, "The probability of life originating from accident is comparable to the probability of the unabridged dictionary resulting from an explosion in a printing factory." I then recited Psalm 19:1. "The heavens declare the glory of God; and the firmament sheweth his handywork." To this I added President Gordon B. Hinckley's testimony: "All of the beauty in the earth bears the fingerprint of the Master Creator."[57]

I continued by sharing 1 Corinthians 2:14: "But the natural man receiveth not the things of the Spirit of God: for they are foolishness unto him: neither can he know them, because they are spiritually discerned."

I explained, "If you rely on your five senses—sight, sound, taste, smell, and touch—you will never know the things of God. A person must experience that sixth sense, the spiritual dimension, to comprehend the divine." I shared, "The things of God are of deep import; and time, and experience, and careful and ponderous and solemn thoughts can only find them out."[58]

He countered with, "If Jesus Christ descended from heaven and stood before me, I would believe."

---

57. Gordon B. Hinckley, "Be Not Faithless," *Ensign*, May 1978, 59.
58. Joseph Smith, *History of the Church*, 3:295.

I remembered how Alma, the Book of Mormon prophet, dealt with Korihor when he sought after a sign. I therefore quoted Alma's response in Alma 30:44, "But Alma said unto him: Thou hast had signs enough; will ye tempt your God? Will ye say, show unto me a sign, when ye have the testimony of all these thy brethren, and also all the holy prophets? The scriptures are laid before thee, yea, and all things denote there is a God; yea, even the earth, and all things that are upon the face of it, yea, and its motion, yea, and also all the planets which move in their regular form do witness that there is a Supreme Creator."

Then I said, "Rather than sight, you need faith. Faith is defined as a belief in things which are not seen but which are true" (see Alma 32:21).

He asked, "How do I develop faith when I don't believe in God?"

I answered, "You begin with a tiny mustard seed of faith." Fortunately, I had Alma 32:26–31 memorized, and I recited it to him.

Now, as I said concerning faith—that it was not a perfect knowledge—even so it is with my words. Ye cannot know of their surety at first, unto perfection, any more than faith is a perfect knowledge.

But behold, if ye will awake and arouse your faculties, even to an experiment upon my words, and exercise a particle of faith, yea, even if ye can no more than desire to believe, let this desire work in you, even until ye believe in a manner that ye can give place for a portion of my words.

Now, we will compare the word unto a seed. Now, if ye give place, that a seed may be planted in your heart, behold, if it be a true seed, or a good seed, if ye do not cast it out by your unbelief, that ye will resist the Spirit of the Lord, behold, it will begin to swell within your breasts; and when you feel these swelling motions, ye will begin to say within yourselves—It must needs be that this is a good seed, or that the word is good, for it beginneth to enlarge my soul; yea, it beginneth to enlighten my understanding, yea, it beginneth to be delicious to me.

Now behold, would not this increase your faith? I say unto you, Yea; nevertheless it hath not grown up to a perfect knowledge.

But behold, as the seed swelleth, and sprouteth, and beginneth to grow, then you must needs say that the seed is good; for behold it swelleth, and sprouteth, and beginneth to grow. And now, behold, will not this strengthen your faith? Yea, it will strengthen your faith: for ye will say I know that this is a good seed; for behold it sprouteth and beginneth to grow.

And now, behold, are ye sure that this is a good seed? I say unto you, Yea; for every seed bringeth forth unto its own likeness.

I taught him, "If you will plant a seed of faith in your heart and not cast it out by your unbelief, but rather cultivate it, nurture it, and if the seed is good, it will grow up into a mighty tree bringing forth its own fruit. Then you will know for yourself that God lives! Take baby steps. 'The creation of a thousand forests is in one acorn.'[59] 'A mighty flame followeth a tiny spark.'"[60]

He nodded in approval, so I pursued it further by questioning, "Do you love your mother?"

He said, "Yes."

"How do you know that you love your mother?"

He was thoughtful and replied, "She has sacrificed everything for me and my family and cares for us deeply, and I have a special feeling for her."

So, I said, "You have experienced love, haven't you?"

He agreed that he had.

I countered, "Has the love you feel for your mother grown over the years?"

He emphatically declared that it had.

I tied our conversation together by sharing, "In the Bible we learn, 'But the fruit of the Spirit is love, joy, peace, longsuffering, gentleness, goodness, and faith'" (Galatians 5:22).

"Love and faith are attributes of God. They will grow and develop within us if we nurture them. 'Faith is a gift of God bestowed as a reward for personal righteousness . . . and the greater the measure of obedience to God's laws, the greater will be the endowment of faith.'[61] I just hope that you'll give faith a try."

Now, what was this atheist's response? He smiled, shook my hand, and said he would like to come to my institute classes. He promised that he would be respectful and just wanted to learn more.

---

59. Ralph Waldo Emerson, *Essays: First Series, History,* 1841, 1.
60. Dante Alighieri, *The Divine Comedy* (New York: New American Library), 2003.
61. Bruce R. McConkie, *Mormon Doctrine,* 264.

18

"I am a child of God" is merely a feel-good idea

Dianne and I were invited to a fundraiser for Foundation for Ancient Research and Mormon Studies, not because we have a lot of money but because the hosts, Alex and Pamela Martinez, knew we would really enjoy it. The FARMS representative was Dr. Daniel C. Peterson, one of the great scholars of our church. He shared a story about a radio talk show pundit in Utah that gave his direct line to bypass the screener and put him onto the show.

One day, while brother Peterson was studying in his library, he heard an anti-Mormon argue, "The Mormons teach 'I am a child of God.' This is a feel-good idea but not doctrine that can be substantiated in the Bible."

Dr. Peterson called the direct line to counter this attack on Church doctrine. He exhorted, "The New Testament does teach that we are all children of God. In Acts 17:29 it reads, 'We are the offspring of God.'"

The anti-Mormon retorted, "The New Testament was written in Greek. If you knew Greek . . . ."

Brother Peterson interrupted, "I have a PhD in Greek."

The antagonist added, "If you had a Greek dictionary, you would find . . . "

Again, Bro. Peterson jumped in with, "I have thirteen Greek dictionaries at my fingertips. Choose one." He began listing off the names of these dictionaries, which I can't even pronounce.

Dr. Peterson explained to all the listeners of the show that offspring in Greek means "family, kin, genes." Indeed, we are the family of God. His genes are in us. I would add Romans 8:16–17, which declares, "The spirit itself beareth witness with our spirit, that we are the children of God: And if children, then heirs; heirs of God, and joint-heirs with Christ."

I'm reminded of the story of a boy who came home from school and asked his mother, "Did I evolve from monkeys?"

She responded, "I don't know. I'm not that familiar with your father's side of the family."

When you know that you are a child of God, you walk taller, reach higher, and are never the same again. *The truth of the matter is that it's in everybody's Bible!*

President Boyd K. Packer said, "You are a child of God. He is the father of your spirit. Spiritually you are of noble birth, the offspring of the king of Heaven. Fix that truth in your mind and hold to it. However many generations in your mortal ancestry, no matter what race or people you represent, the pedigree of your spirit can be written on a single line. You are a child of God!"[62]

---

62. *Let Not Your Heart Be Troubled,* 50.

19

Where did you gentlemen get the authority to organize a church in our town?

I took my wife to dinner at Rubio's on Taco Tuesday for $1.49 fish tacos. I also got a cup of water with lemon. As you can see, it was a big night on the town.

While we were eating, I heard the conversation in the booth behind us. Two young men were preparing to start a church in San Clemente, California, and were receiving counsel from an adviser. They discussed how many square feet they needed for their building, who would do their printing, what their budget was for advertising, where they would get their pews, how much in offerings they needed each week to be profitable, and so on. The advisor mentioned every expense necessary to get started so they knew how much money they needed to acquire to begin their church.

When Dianne and I finished our meal, I stopped at their table and said, "I couldn't help but overhear that you young men are starting a new church. I wish you well in your ministry. I just have one question."

They responded enthusiastically, "What is it?"

I stated, "In Hebrews 5:4 we read, 'And no man taketh this honor unto himself, but he that is called of God, as was Aaron.' In Exodus 28:1 we learn that Aaron was called of God through the prophet Moses."

I asked them, "Where did you gentlemen get the authority to organize a church in our town?"

They thought for a moment and broke the silence by saying they received a diploma from Chapman University Divinity School.

I recited to them the words of Elder Bruce R. McConkie: "Jesus never attended a theological seminary; he never graduated from a divinity school; he was not trained for the ministry in the traditional sense; his religious learning was not born of the wisdom of men—and such was true of the fishermen and others whom he called to hold the keys of his earthly kingdom. None of them would have qualified as sectarian ministers or a Jewish Rabbis, but all of them were called of God and held his authority."[63] *"The Truth of the Matter is that it's in everybody's Bible!"*

They looked at one another, they looked at their advisor, then they looked back at me and each other again. Their eyes got bigger and a look of panic overcame them.

My wife said sweetly, "Come on, honey, let's go."

---

63. Bruce R. McConkie, *Doctrinal New Testament Commentary*, Vol. 1, 441.

20

The holy garments of salvation

I participated on a panel to answer questions posed by 150 young single adults not of our faith. The moderator collected the written questions from the audience. One of the questions he asked me was, "What's with the magic underwear that Mormons wear?"

Some in the audience laughed. I answered kindly, "Latter-day Saints receive the same ordinance in the temple today that Aaron and his sons received in the ancient Tabernacle. 'And thou shalt bring Aaron and his sons unto the door of the tabernacle of the congregation, and wash them with water. And thou shalt put upon Aaron the holy garments, and anoint him, and sanctify him' (Exodus 40:12–13). The Lord described them as 'holy garments.' In Isaiah 61:10 they are referred to as the 'garments of salvation.' We are counseled in the scriptures not to trifle with sacred things. To irreverently refer to the holy garments of salvation as magic underwear is offensive to the Lord and to members of The Church of Jesus Christ of Latter-day Saints.

"Secondly, in Genesis 3:21 we learn, 'Unto Adam also and to his wife did the Lord God make coats of skins, and clothed them.'" I explained, "To cover Adam and Eve in coats of skins required the shedding of blood and the death of the animal. This is in similitude of the Atonement of Jesus Christ. The Hebrew word for atone, *Khofar*, means to cover. When I put on my garments every day, I am covered in the Atonement of Jesus Christ as a protection from sin.

"Additionally, the Savior said, 'Take heed that ye do not your alms before men, to be seen of them: otherwise ye have no reward of your Father which is in heaven' (Matthew 6:1). Latter-day Saints do not wear signs and symbols to show others that we are Christians. We humbly wear our garments beneath our clothing and show the world we are Christian by our countenance and conduct.

"Church members ask for the same degree of respect and sensitivity that would be afforded religious vestments of other faiths: the nun's habit, the priest's cassock, the Jewish prayer shawl, the Muslim's skullcap, and the saffron robes of the Buddhist monk."

21

When I go on vacation, will you be the minister for the day to my Unitarian congregation?

I represented our church on a panel with leaders of other churches at the Religions Diversity Fair on the University of California—Irvine campus. The moderator was a Unitarian minister in Mission Viejo, California. When he went on vacation during the summer, he asked me to be the "minister-for-the-day" to his congregation. I readily accepted the invitation and asked, "What do you want me to teach?"

He said, "Tell them what you believe."

I inquired, "Do you want me to explain the fundamental doctrines of our church and how I know they are true?"

He answered, "That's exactly what I want you to do."

"Do you want me to tone it down a little bit from the way I usually preach?"

He shot back, "No way. Tell it to us straight."

"So, you want me to come out with both guns blazing?"

"Yes, don't hold back at all."

I asked if he had a youth minister to teach the children. He indicated that they did, so I asked his permission to teach the children, which he gave me. I knew I would win the hearts of the parents if I could inspire their children. For a visual aid, I took a rubber rattlesnake and told the following story:

Many years ago, Indian braves would go away in solitude to prepare for manhood. One hiked into a beautiful valley, green with trees, bright with flowers. There, as he looked up at the surrounding mountains, he noticed one rugged peak, capped with dazzling snow.

"I will test myself against that mountain," he thought. He put on his buffalo-hide shirt, threw his blanket over his shoulders and set off to climb the pinnacle.

When he reached the top, he stood on the rim of the world. He could see forever, and his heart swelled with pride. Then he heard a rustle at his feet. Looking down he saw a snake. Before he could move, the snake spoke.

"I am about to die," said the snake. "It is too cold for me up here, and there is no food. Put me under your shirt and take me down to the valley."

"No," said the youth. "I know your kind. You are a rattlesnake. If I pick you up you will bite and your bite will kill me."

"Not so," said the snake. "I will treat you differently. If you do this for me, I will not harm you."

The youth resisted awhile, but this was a very persuasive snake. At last the youth tucked it under his shirt and carried it down to the valley. There he laid it down gently. Suddenly the snake coiled, rattled and leaped, biting him on the leg.

"But you promised," cried the youth.

"You knew what I was when you picked me up," said the snake as it slithered away.

And now, wherever I go, I tell that story to young people who might be tempted by drugs. Remember the words of the snake: "You knew what I was when you picked me up."[64] I encouraged the youth to abstain from drugs and alcohol.

The children were captivated and the parents were delighted. When the forty or so children were escorted to Sunday School, I gazed upon the adults and thought to myself, "Now you're really gonna get it!"

Interestingly, there was a gentleman in a booth that controlled the lighting and music. My voice intensifies as I become more passionate. Accordingly, when my volume would crescendo, the stage manager increased the sound and adjusted the lighting to a reddish hue. A tenant of their faith is that they readily accept truth from whatever source it comes. Knowing this, I began by quoting Brigham Young, who said, "Mormonism embraces all truth that is revealed and that is unrevealed, whether religious, political, scientific, or philosophical."[65] They were shocked to learn that it is also a tenant of our faith.

I taught them the Apostasy, First Vision, coming forth of the Book of Mormon, restoration of the priesthood, and seventeen points of the

---

64. "Iron Eyes Cody," *Readers Digest*, June 1989, 131.
65. Brigham Young, *Journal of Discourses*, 9:149.

true church. At the conclusion of the service, the associate pastor and I shook hands with every member of the congregation. They responded most favorably to my discourse. Honestly, I thought they would never ask me to come back. To my surprise, two years later, the Unitarians invited me to teach them again. It was awesome!

22

I don't need Joseph Smith and his successors. All I need is in the Bible.

I went to the gym the day following the 2007 not-so "Special on the Mormons" that aired on PBS Television. It showed a definite bias against the Church. I encountered a friend I nicknamed Muscle Mike. He exercises three hours every day in a tank top because if he scratched his head while wearing a T-shirt, it would rip. Muscle Mike, who is a born-again saved Christian, said to me, "I watched the PBS program on the Mormons last night. I don't need Joseph Smith and his successors. All that I need is in the Bible."

Five or six burly bodybuilders overheard our discussion and suspended their workout to listen in. I shared with them three inspirational statements about the Prophet Joseph Smith that I had memorized:

> It was decreed in the councils of eternity, long before the foundations of the earth were laid, that he, Joseph Smith, should be the man, in the last dispensation of this world, to bring forth the word of God to the people, and receive the fullness of the keys and power of the Priesthood of the Son of God. . . . He was foreordained in eternity to preside over this last dispensation.[66]

> [Joseph Smith] prophesied. He taught gospel principles. He translated. He brought forth books of scripture—both ancient and modern. He built temples and cities. He was a revealer of the knowledge of Christ. He was the authorized servant of God. He fulfilled every requirement to complete the profile of a prophet. In due time Joseph received the Keys of the Kingdom. With this apostolic power he re-established the true Church in its fullness and power. The Lord said to him, " . . . this generation shall have my word through you" (D&C 5:10). There is no greater prophet in any dispensation than Joseph Smith. He translated the Book of

---

66. *Discourses of Brigham Young*, 108; JD 7:289–90.

Mormon from ancient plates. Its purpose is to be another witness that Jesus is the Christ. Concerning this book, the Lord declared: "And he has translated the book, even that part which I have commanded him, and as your Lord and your God liveth it is true!" (D&C 17:6).[67]

His work will live to endless ages, and unnumbered millions yet unborn will mention his name with honor, as a noble instrument in the hands of God, who, during his short and youthful career, laid the foundation of that kingdom spoken of by Daniel, the prophet, which should break in pieces all other kingdoms and stand forever.[68]

I testified, "God is the same yesterday, today, and forever and He speaks through a living prophet in our day and age just as he did in ancient times. He is the Great I AM, not the Great He Was. He *speaketh*, not *spake*."

Muscle Mike and his jumbo comrades stared at me with their mouths wide open. I looked them in the eye, smiled brightly, and gave them a fist bump. Then I turned around, walked over to the bench press, and resumed my vain attempt to resurrect a sunken chest.

---

67. A. Theodore Tuttle, *Church News*, 17 March 2001.
68. *Autobiography of Parley P. Pratt*, 1979, 46.

23

Joseph Smith's prophecy that the New Jerusalem temple would be reared in this generation was not fulfilled. Doesn't this expose him as a false prophet? Hasn't modern DNA research proved that the Book of Mormon is false?

A young man named Jared called me and said, "I was told you could answer my questions. I left the Church six years ago and asked to have my name removed from the records. Can we meet?"

His best friend's family attends an evangelical church, and they continually attacked our religion until he eventually lost his faith. He had been dating and fell in love with a faithful young woman named Stacey. I was her bishop when she was a little girl. She had told Jared that she would never settle for anything less than a temple marriage. With the prospect of losing her, he realized he must find out once and for all if there were answers to the questions that troubled him.

Under these circumstances, when confronted with highly technical questions, I always meet at my Institute of Religion, where I have more than two hundred books and file cabinets full of my reference material.

Question #1:

"Joseph Smith prophesied that the temple in the New Jerusalem would be reared in this generation (see D&C 84:4). Moses recorded, 'When a prophet speaketh in the name of the Lord, if the thing follow not, nor come to pass, that is the thing which the Lord hath not spoken, but the prophet hath spoken it presumptuously: thou shalt not be afraid of him' (Deuteronomy 18:22). Because this prophecy was not fulfilled, doesn't this expose Joseph Smith as a false prophet?"

I recited Matthew 16:4: "A wicked and adulterous generation seeketh after a sign."

"This generation did not have reference to a period of years, but to a period of wickedness. A generation may mean the time of this present dispensation."[69]

Doctrine and Covenants 124:49–51 explains, "Verily, verily, I say unto you, that when I give a commandment to any of the sons of men to do a work unto my name, and those sons of men go with all their might and with all they have to perform that work, and cease not their diligence, and their enemies come upon them and hinder them from performing that work, behold, it behooveth me to require that work no more at the hands of those sons of men, but to accept of their offerings. And the iniquity and transgression of my holy laws and commandments I will visit upon the heads of those who hindered my work, unto the third and fourth generation, so long as they repent not, and hate me, saith the Lord God."

I asked Jared, "Who was it that hindered the Lord's work and will have God's wrath upon his head?" He didn't know. My answer was, "Governor Boggs of Missouri, who issued the extermination order: 'The Mormons must be treated as enemies and must be exterminated or driven from the state.'"

I added, "'I the Lord command and revoke, as it seemeth me good' (D&C 56:4). For example, the Lord revoked His command to Moses. After promising Moses and the Israelites that they would enter the promised land, the Lord said, 'Your carcases shall fall in this wilderness; and all that were numbered of you, according to your whole number, from twenty years old and upward, which have murmured against me. Doubtless ye shall not come into the land, concerning which I sware to make you dwell therein. . . . After the number of the days in which ye searched the land, even forty days, each day for a year, shall ye bear your iniquities, even forty years, and ye shall know my breach of promise' (Numbers 14:29–30,34). The *American Heritage Dictionary* defines 'breach of promise' as 'the failure to fulfill a promise.'"

Another example I shared comes from the Messianic prophet Isaiah. Isaiah came to Hezekiah and said, "Thus saith the Lord, set thine house in order; for thou shalt die and not live." Following this devastating prophesy by Isaiah, the Lord said, "Tell Hezekiah . . . thus

69. See Joseph Fielding Smith, *Answers to Gospel Questions*, vol. 4, 111.

saith the Lord God . . . I will heal thee . . . and I will add unto thy days fifteen years" (2 Kings 20:1–7).

Additionally, the Lord promised to destroy Nineveh because of their wickedness. However, "God repented of the evil, that he had said that he would do unto them, and he did it not" (see Jonah 3:1–5, 10).

I explained to Jared, "If one rejects the Prophet Joseph Smith because the temple in Missouri has not yet been built, then by this same reasoning, one would necessarily have to conclude that Moses was a false prophet because he failed to lead the Israelites into the promised land; regard Isaiah as a false prophet because his prophecy that Hezekiah would die did not come to pass; and not accept Jonah for prophesying that Nineveh would be destroyed."

I then reviewed with Jared some of the prophecies made by the Prophet Joseph Smith:

> On Sunday night the Prophet called on all who held the Priesthood to gather into the little log school house they had there. It was a small house, perhaps 14 feet square. But it held the whole of the Priesthood of The Church of Jesus Christ of Latter-day Saints who were then in the town of Kirtland, and who had gathered together to go off in Zion's Camp. That was the first time I ever saw Oliver Cowdery, or heard him speak; the first time I ever saw Brigham Young and Heber C. Kimball, and the two Pratts, and Orson Hyde and many others. There were no Apostles in the Church then except Joseph Smith and Oliver Cowdery. When we got together the Prophet called upon the Elders of Israel with him to bear testimony of this work. Those that I have named spoke and a good many that I have not named, bore their testimonies. When they got through the Prophet said, "Brethren, I have been very much edified and instructed in your testimonies here tonight, but I want to say to you before the Lord, that you know no more concerning the destinies of this Church and kingdom than a babe upon its mother's lap. You don't comprehend it." I was rather surprised. He said, "It is only a little handful of Priesthood you see here tonight, but this Church will fill North and South America—it will fill the world." Among other things he said, "It will fill the Rocky Mountains. There will be tens of thousands of Latter-day Saints who will be gathered in the Rocky Mountains, and there they will open the door for the establishing of the gospel among the Lamanites, who will receive

the gospel and their endowments and the blessings of God. This people will go into the Rocky Mountains; they will there build temples to the Most High. They will raise up a posterity there, and the Latter-day Saints who dwell in these mountains will stand in the flesh until the coming of the Son of Man. The Son of Man will come to them while in the Rocky Mountains."

I name these things because I want to bear testimony before God, angels and men that mine eyes behold the day, and have beheld for the last fifty years of my life, the fulfillment of that prophecy.[70]

I had a conversation with a number of brethren in the shade of the building on the subject of our persecutions in Missouri and the constant annoyance which has followed us since we were driven from that state. I prophesied that the Saints would continue to suffer much affliction and would be driven to the Rocky Mountains: many would apostatize, others would be put to death by our persecutors or lose their lives in consequence of exposure or disease, and some of you will live to go and assist in making settlements and build cities and see the Saints become a mighty people in the heart of the Rocky Mountains.

[Among those present when this prediction was uttered was Elder Anson Call, who has left on record additional details respecting this remarkable prediction. He says that in the shade of the building mentioned was a barrel of ice water, and the men were drinking it to quench their thirst on the hot August day. Following is Anson's account:]

With the tumbler still in his hand he prophesied that the Saints would go to the Rocky Mountains: and, said he, "this water tastes much like that of the crystal streams that are running from the snowcapped mountains. . . ." I had before seen him in a vision and now saw while he was talking his countenance changed to white, not the deadly white of a bloodless face, but a living brilliant white. He seemed absorbed in gazing at something at a great distance and said: 'I am gazing upon the valleys of those mountains.' This was followed by a vivid description of the scenery of these mountains as I have since become acquainted with it.

---

70. Wilford Woodruff, in Conference Report, April 1898, 57.

Pointing to Shadrach Roundy and others he said: "There are some men here who shall do a great work in that land.' Pointing to me, he said: 'There is Anson, he shall go and shall assist in building up cities from one end of the country to the other and you,' rather extending the idea to all those he had spoken of, 'shall perform as great a work as has been done by man; so that the nations of the earth shall be astonished; and many of them will be gathered in that land and assist in building cities and temples and Israel shall be made to rejoice."

It was impossible to represent in words this scene, which is still vivid in my mind, of the grandeur of Joseph's appearance, his beautiful descriptions of this land and his wonderful prophetic utterances as they emanated from the glorious inspiration that overshadowed him.[71]

May 18th, 1843—Joseph Smith dined with Judge Stephen A. Douglas, who was presiding at court.

"Judge, you will aspire to the presidency of the United States; and if you ever turn your hand against me or the Latter-day Saints, you will feel the weight of the hand of the Almighty upon you; and you will live to see and know that I have testified the truth to you; for the conversation of this day will stick to you through life."

Fourteen years after the interview containing the prophecy, Mr. Douglas was called upon to deliver a speech in Springfield, the capitol of Illinois. His speech was published in the Missouri Republican of June 18, 1857. It was well known that Mr. Douglas had been on terms of intimate friendship with President Joseph Smith, and was well acquainted with the other church leaders. He was therefore looked upon as one competent to speak upon the "Mormon" question, and was invited to do so in the speech. Mr. Douglas addressed the Mormon question and concluded: "Let us have these facts in an official shape before the president and congress, and the country will soon learn that, in the performance of the high and solemn duty devolving upon the executive and congress, there will be no vacillating or hesitating policy. It will be as prompt as the peal that follows the flash—as stern and unyielding as death. Should such a state of things actually exist as we are led to

---

71. Joseph Smith, *History of the Church*, 5:85–86.

infer from the reports—and such information comes in an official shape—the knife must be applied to this pestiferous, disgusting cancer, which is gnawing into the very vitals of the body politic. It must be cut out by the roots and seared over by the red-hot iron of stern and unflinching law.

A lengthy review of Mr. Douglas' speech was published in the editorial columns of the Deseret News in the issue of that paper for September 2, 1857, addressed directly to Mr. Douglas. The closing paragraph includes the following: "Inasmuch as you were well acquainted with Joseph Smith, and this people, also with the character of our maligners, and did know their allegations were false; and also that you may thoroughly understand that you have voluntarily, knowingly, and of choice sealed your damnation, and by your own chosen course have closed your chance for the presidential chair, through disobeying the counsel of Joseph which you formerly sought and prospered by following, and that you in common with us, may testify to all the world that Joseph was a true prophet, the following extract from the history of Joseph Smith is again printed for your benefit, and is kindly recommended to your careful perusal and most candid consideration.

There follows the excerpt from history we have already read. When Mr. Douglas first began to aspire to the presidency, no man in the history of American politics had more reason to hope for success. The political party of which he was the recognized leader, in the preceding presidential election had polled 174 electoral votes as against 122 cast by the other two parties which opposed it, and a popular vote of 1,838,169 as against 1,215,798 votes for the two parties opposing. It is a matter of history, however, that the Democratic party in the election of 1860 was badly divided; and factions of it put candidates into the field with the following result: Abraham Lincoln, candidate of the Republican party, was triumphantly elected. He received 180 electoral votes; Mr. Breckenridge received 72 electoral votes; Mr. Bell 38; and Mr. Douglas 12. "By a plurality count of the popular vote, Mr. Lincoln carried 18 states; Mr. Breckenridge 11; Mr. Bell 3; and Mr. Douglas one—Missouri! Less than one year after his nomination by the Baltimore Convention, only forty-eight years of age, Mr. Douglas died at his home in Chicago."[72]

On December 25, 1832, Joseph Smith received Doctrine and Covenants 87, a revelation and prophecy on war. "Verily, thus saith the Lord concerning the wars that will shortly come to pass, beginning at the rebellion of South Carolina, which will eventually terminate in the death and misery of many souls; And the time will come that war will be poured out upon all nations, beginning at this place. For behold, the Southern States shall be divided against the Northern States, and the Southern States will call on other nations, even the nation of Great Britain, as it is called, and they shall also call upon other nations, in order to defend themselves against other nations; and then war shall be poured out upon all nations" (D&C 87:1–3).

"On the 12th of April 1861, the first shot of the war was fired by General Beauregard against Fort Sumter, and thus the conflict was begun by South Carolina, as foretold by the Prophet, and not by any of the Northern States.

"It was a war that brought death and misery to many souls. The entire loss on both sides, including deaths from diseases and wounds, is estimated at a million men."[73]

"The Prophet Joseph gave us this marvelous revelation in 1832. The Civil War came in 1861; the war between Denmark and Prussia in 1864; Italy and Austria in 1865 and 1866; Austria and Prussia in 1866; Russia and Turkey in 1877; China and Japan in 1894 and 1895; Spanish-American in 1898; Japan and Russia in 1904 and 1905; World War I in 1914–1918; then the next war was a comparatively small one, Ethiopia and Italy. . . . Then, the World War [World War II], and . . . the Korean War. [Since 1958 there have been, among numerous other wars, the Vietnam War in Southeast Asia, the war in Angola, and the Six-Day and Yom Kippur wars in the Holy Land.]"[74]

Add to these the war between England and Argentina, the Soviet Union and Afghanistan, the Civil War in Rwanda, the Bosnian War, and the two Persian Gulf Wars.

---

72. *Deseret News,* September 2, 1857
73. Hyrum M. Smith and Janne M. Sjodahl, *Doctrine and Covenants Commentary,* 535.
74. Joseph L. Wirthlin, in Conference Report, October 1958, 33.

I informed him that the Old Testament Prophet Jeremiah testified, "When the word of the prophet shall come to pass, then shall the prophet be known that the Lord hath truly sent him" (Jeremiah 28:9). Joseph Smith made more than 100 prophecies that were all fulfilled.

Question #2:

"How do you answer the critics who have stated that modern DNA research has conclusively proved that the Book of Mormon is false?"

In April 1929, President Anthony W. Ivins (counselor in the First Presidency) said in general conference: "The Book of Mormon teaches the history of three distinct peoples . . . who came from the old world to this continent. It does not tell us that there was no one here before them. It does not tell us that people did not come after."

In a very real sense, this debate is (or should be) over. Simon Southerton, an Australian plant geneticist and former Latter-day Saint who is now the most vocal critic of the Book of Mormon on DNA grounds, admitted, "In 600 BC there were probably several million American Indians living in the Americas. If a small group of Israelites, say less than thirty, entered such a massive native population, it would be very hard to detect their genes today."[75]

"In the June 2003 issue of the *American Journal of Human Genetics*, scientists performed a DNA study compared with the extensive genealogies from 131,060 people of Iceland. This was probably the most massive population study ever performed. This test showed that the majority of people living today in Iceland had ancestors living only 150 years ago that could not be detected based on the Y-chromosome and Mitochondrial DNA tests being performed and yet the genealogical records exist showing that these people lived and were real ancestors."[76]

After 90 minutes I asked Jared if he had time for me to share one more story. He consented.

---

75. Daniel C. Peterson, *The Book of Mormon and DNA Research*, xii.
76. farms.byu.edu/publications/dna/ButlerBofMandDNA_Feb2006.php.

In a local newspaper in Provo, Utah, there had been an ongoing series of articles written by individuals who wanted to persuade LDS church members to leave the Church. In response to the highly critical and spirited remarks, a local member wrote this rebuttal:

Editor:

I have been thinking of quitting the Mormon Church. Yes, if I can, I am going to get even with that church. As soon as I can find another church that teaches about the Gathering of the House of Israel; the return of the Jews to Palestine; the building of temples and what they do in them; the mission of Elijah, the prophet, as predicted by Malachi; the explanation of the three degrees of glory (three heavens) as mentioned by Paul; the restoration of the gospel by modern revelation as promised by Peter and Paul and Jesus himself; the belief in eternity; that teaches abstinence from all harmful drugs and beverages; that sells the best fire insurance policy on earth, for the last days for only a 10th of my income – and that clothes and feeds its members and many non-members throughout the world.

Yes, sir, as soon as I find another church that teaches all that, or even half as much, I will say goodbye to this Mormon Church. The church that I am looking for must also be able to motivate 50,000 youth and adults to leave their homes for two years at their own expense and go to far-away places to teach and preach without salary. Yes, it must also teach and show why salvation is assured for children who die before eight years of age.

Mr. Editor, could you help me find a church that teaches all that and more than a hundred other doctrines and principles, which I have no room to mention here, and which brings solace, comfort to the soul, peace, hope and salvation to mankind, and above all, that answers the key questions that all the great philosophers have asked; the meaning of life, the purpose of death, suffering and pain; the absolute need for a Redeemer and the marvelous plan revealed and executed by Jesus Christ the Savior? Yes, as soon as I find another church that teaches and also has the organization and the Priesthood authority to perform the saving ordinances of the gospel, I am going to quit the Mormon Church, for I should not tolerate that "they" should change a few words in Book of Mormon—even if those changes simply improve the grammar and the syntax of the verses. . . .

So, I repeat, if any one of the kind readers of this letter knows about another church that teaches and does as much for mankind as the Mormon church, please let me know. And please do it soon, because my turn to go to the cannery is coming up. Also "they" want my last son – the fifth one – to go away for two years on a mission, and again, I have to pay for all that. I have heard that our ward is going to be divided again, and it is our side that must build the new chapel. And also, someone the other day had the gall of suggesting that my wife and I get ready to go on a second mission, and when you come back you can volunteer as a temple worker. Boy, these Mormons don't leave you alone for a minute. And what do I get for all that, I asked? "Well," they said, "for one you can look forward to a funeral service at no charge." . . . Do you think you can help me find another church?"[77]

What was the result of our hour-and-a-half visit? Jared has come back to church. He has proposed to Stacey. He is being interviewed by the bishop to receive the Melchizedek Priesthood. His father called me and said, "My son said that you talked today and answered his questions. Thank you for helping to rescue my son."

---

77. Letter to the Editor: "Find Me a Better Church," *Central Utah Journal*, 1982 (author's name withheld).

24

"Now I know what hell would be like"

While serving as the mission president's assistant, my companion and I regularly teamed up with the Elders to visit and teach their investigators. One gentleman we contacted had been through scores of missionaries. He enjoyed confounding and running circles around us with his superior knowledge of the Bible. I asked him to tell me about his wife. He responded, "If there is anyone in the LDS Church that will go to the celestial kingdom, it's my wife. She is the best Christian woman I have ever known!"

I asked him, "Don't you desire to be sealed to your wife and children in the temple so that you can be together for time and eternity rather than 'until death do you part'?"

His answer surprised me. Said he, "After I die, if I get to the other side and find out that the Church is really true, my wife will do my ordinance work in the temple. So why should I join the Church now and be expected to change my lifestyle?"

President Lorenzo Snow said, "There is a way to reach every human heart, and it is your business to find the way to the hearts of those to whom you are called on this mission."[78]

I said a silent prayer for inspiration. I had a prompting to have him read D&C 132:39. The only problem was that I had no idea what was contained in that verse. But acting on faith I asked him to read that specific reference. I know the Lord blessed me because I never would have thought to use a plural marriage reference as a baptismal challenge on my own. "In none of these things did he [David] sin against me save in the case of Uriah and his wife; and, therefore he hath fallen from his exaltation, and received his portion; and he shall not inherit them out of the world, for I gave them unto another, saith the Lord."

I then asked him, "How would you feel if your wife and children were given unto another more valiant disciple in the next world

---

78. *The Teachings of Lorenzo Snow*, edited by Clyde J. Williams, 66–8.

because you refused to repent and be baptized and faithfully follow the Savior Jesus Christ?"

He pondered my question for a long time. I knew it would be a mistake to say anything more. He read the verse again and again, and finally with tears in his eyes broke the silence by saying, "Now I know what hell would be like!" This good man humbled himself and listened to our message "with a sincere heart, with real intent, having faith in Christ" (See Moroni 10:4).

25

When you see the wounds in the Savior's hands, what will you say to Him then?

I received a phone call from a close friend, who asked if I would do him a favor. I replied, "Of course, Steve, I'll do anything for you."

He said, "We have always wanted to go to the Holy Land, but we will only go if you and Dianne join us."

I explained that Dianne and I had not budgeted for such a trip.

He replied, "You don't understand. All expenses will be paid, but we won't go without you."

I quickly responded, "As I said, Steve, I'll do anything for you." This was a trip never to be forgotten, to walk where Jesus walked.

One of our excursions was to Armageddon, the Valley of Jezreel, sixty miles north of Jerusalem at the ancient city of Megiddo. I asked our Jewish tour guide, Eli, "What is your understanding of the Battle of Armageddon?"

He answered, "I believe it will be a war of words, but not a war with weapons."

I requested he read Zechariah 14:2–3: "For I will gather all nations against Jerusalem to battle; and the city shall be taken, and the houses rifled, and the women ravished; and half of the city shall go forth into captivity, and the residue of the people shall not be cut off from the city. Then shall the Lord go forth, and fight against those nations, as when he fought in the day of battle."

I then invited him to read verse 12. "The Lord will smite all the people that have fought against Jerusalem; Their flesh shall consume away while they stand upon their feet, and their eyes shall consume away in their holes, and their tongue shall consume away in their mouth."

I said to Eli, "This sounds to me like nuclear, chemical, and biological weapons. Ezekiel prophesied that it would take seven years to burn the discarded weapons of war with fire. And seven months to bury the dead to cleanse the land" (see Ezekiel 39:9, 12). I added, "These are your Jewish prophets, Zechariah and Ezekiel, in your book, the Old Testament! But I have one more question for you. Will you examine Zechariah 13:6?"

"And one shall say unto him, What are these wounds in thine hands? Then he shall answer, Those with which I was wounded in the house of my friends."

I inquired, "When Jesus Christ comes in power and great glory to save His people Israel at the height of the Battle of Armageddon, and you see the wounds in His hands, what will you say to him then?"

The silence was deafening!

26

The law of tithing specifies a particularly profound, prophetic promise

While serving as stake public affairs director, I was assigned to give Rabbi Krause and his entourage of Jewish leaders a tour of the Laguna Niguel California Stake Center. They used our stake center to accommodate the large number of worshipers that come out for their "High and Holy Days." Our Church in Laguna has two stories, two chapels, two kitchens, a full-length basketball court, and a stage. As we walked through the edifice they marveled at its beauty.

At the conclusion of our walk-through, we stood at the grand staircase under a chandelier. The group asked, "How can you people afford such a spectacular church building as this?"

I answered, "Actually, we have you to thank." Their inquisitive expressions beckoned me to continue. "The Lord has specified a particularly, profound, prophetic promise in your Old Testament: 'Will a man rob God? Yet ye have robbed me. But ye say, Wherein have we robbed thee? In tithes and offerings. Ye are cursed with a curse: for ye have robbed me, even this whole nation. Bring ye all the tithes into the storehouse, that there may be meat in mine house, and prove me now herewith, saith the Lord of hosts, if I will not open you the windows of heaven, and pour you out a blessing, that there shall not be room enough to receive it'" (Malachi 3:8–10).

The look on their faces as they looked at each other said it all. "We don't have a synagogue of sufficient size to provide for our people on our holiest holidays. We turn to our LDS friends who have applied the law of tithing in our scriptures, and they have been greatly blessed because of their obedience."

27

We have come to listen to a prophet's voice and hear the word of God

President Spencer W. Kimball addressed about 15,000 youth in the Long Beach, California, area. I was teaching seminary at the time, and some of their parents and I brought several carloads of my students to hear the prophet. As we approached the sports arena, we noticed a number of people passing out anti-Mormon literature. I decided to ignore these antagonists and continue inside to secure seats. When we attempted to walk past them, a young man grabbed me by the arm, struck me in the face with a pamphlet, and made several offensive remarks about the Church.

I tried to avoid confrontation, but he forced the issue, and with my students standing there, I felt it necessary to defend our faith. I said to this fellow, "Look at these young people. They're happy, clean-cut, virtuous, and they don't smoke, drink, or take drugs. They get up about 5:30 every morning to study the scriptures in seminary for an hour before going to school. They love the Lord and strive to keep His commandments. The Savior said, 'Suffer the little children to come unto me, and forbid them not: for of such is the kingdom of God'" (Mark 10:14).

I then pointed to a theatre across the street and asked, "Do you see the type of film that is being shown there?" The movie had an X rating. I then said to this fellow, "Rather than obstructing these youth from hearing the gospel, why don't you go across the street and discourage people from viewing those vulgar and immoral movies? Instead of attempting to destroy the faith of these wholesome teenagers, why don't you redirect the lives of those carnal souls who have strayed from the strait and narrow path?" He had nothing to say, so I testified, "We have come to listen to a prophet's voice and hear the word of God."

28

Why do you reject the creeds when they are clearly taught in the Bible and Book of Mormon?

While working at the Mission Viejo, California, Institute of Religion, I received an anonymous phone call. The caller immediately got to his point. "Why do you reject the creeds when they are clearly taught in the Bible and Book of Mormon?" He then referred to the Testimony of the Three Witnesses. "And the honor be to the Father, and to the Son, and to the Holy Ghost, which is one God. Amen." Next, he read 2 Nephi 31:21, "This is the doctrine of Christ, and the only and true doctrine of the Father, and of the Son, and of the Holy Ghost, which is one God, without end. Amen." Finally, he shared 3 Nephi 11:27. "I say unto you, that the Father, and the Son, and the Holy Ghost are one; and I am in the Father, and the Father in me, and the Father and I are one."

I answered simply, "God and Christ are literally a Father and a Son—separate, distinct, individual beings who are wholly unified in their purpose."[79]

I invited him to read John 17:20–22: "Neither pray I for these alone, but for them also which shall believe on me through their word; That they all may be one; as thou, Father, art in me, and I in thee, that they also may be one in us: that the world may believe that thou hast sent me. And the glory which thou gavest me I have given them; that they may be one, even as we are one." I explained, "If the apostles become one with the Father, Son, and Holy Ghost we no longer have a Trinity but a Fifteenity. Certainly, the Lord was praying for His disciples to be unified."

"These creeds declare the Father, Son, and Holy Ghost to be abstract, absolute, transcendent, imminent, consubstantial, coeternal, and unknowable, without body, parts or passions and dwelling outside

---

79. Robert D. Hales, "Eternal Life—to Know Our Heavenly Father and His Son, Jesus Christ," *Ensign*, Nov. 2014.

space and time . . . the oft noted 'mystery of the trinity.' They are three distinct persons, yet not three Gods but one."[80]

I asked this gentleman if he had studied the history behind the Nicene Creed. He admitted that he had not done his homework on this subject. I shared, "Constantine was the emperor of Rome. Having fought a long civil war, he felt that a state religion, as popular as Christianity had become, would help him solidify his empire. Making it the favorite religion of the state gave to him influence in the operation of the church. He called a council of all bishops under his control in 325 A.D. to settle the dispute over the doctrine of the nature of God. Athanasius maintained that there were three co-equal Gods in one substance, and Arius argued that Christ was of a distinct substance from and came after the Father. Constantine favored the Athanasian side. The Aryans who still objected were banished, and he appointed new bishops in place of them. And by what authority? He had none. He acted as emperor, and the authority by which he appointed these bishops was political, not divine. They became appointees of Constantine, not of the Lord. In this Nicene Council, Constantine—uninspired, un-baptized, still a sun worshiper, a man who committed murder within his own family, by his political power—took the steps which gave to later Christianity its doctrine concerning the nature of God whom they worshiped."[81]

I informed him that *Harper's Bible Dictionary*, which is at seminaries across America, records that "the formal doctrine of the Trinity as it was defined by the great church councils of the fourth and fifth centuries is not to be found in the [New Testament]."[82]

I probed, "Have I answered your question?"

He indicated that I had done so.

I continued, "May I put a question to you similar to the one you asked me?" He agreed, so I inquired, "Why do you accept the creeds when the Bible clearly teaches that the Godhead are separate and distinct beings?"

He responded, "What do you mean?"

---

80. Jeffrey R. Holland, in Conference Report, October 2007.
81. See Mark E. Peterson, *Which Church Is Right*.
82. Elder Jeffrey R. Holland, in Conference Report, October 2007.

I quoted Matthew 3:16–17: "Jesus, when he was baptized, went up straightway out of the water: and, lo, the heavens were opened unto him, and he saw the Spirit of God descending like a dove, and lighting upon him: And lo a voice from heaven, saying, This is my beloved Son, in whom I am well pleased." I asked him, "Where was Jesus baptized?"

He said, "In the river Jordan."

"Who descended like a dove and lit upon Him?"

"The Holy Ghost."

"Whose voice was heard from heaven declaring, 'This is my beloved Son?'"

He answered, "It was God the Father."

"The truth of the matter is that it's in everybody's Bible!" I explained, "Now you understand the nature of the Godhead."

My caller thanked me, and I invited him to take the missionary lessons and learn more about the Church.

29

Some people believe Mormonism is a cult

Tory, a sweet institute student who is a recent convert, shared a terrible experience she had in a class at Saddleback College. The students were asked to write about something that made them sad. She explained that her parents are unhappy and very critical because of her baptism into the Church. The teacher stated to the entire class, "I can understand why they feel that way. Some people believe Mormonism is a cult!"

When Tory arrived at institute that day, I could tell immediately that she was distraught. We sat down together, and she shared the reason she was upset. From the Book of Mormon we read, "At that day shall he rage in the hearts of the children of men, and stir them up to anger against that which is good" (2 Nephi 28:20). I testified that The Church of Jesus Christ of Latter-day Saints and everything about it is good. Isaiah recorded, "Woe unto them that call evil good and good evil." (Isaiah 5:20)

Because we were in the institute building, I could access my office files. I shared with Tory an excellent response to this insulting accusation written by BYU religion professor Daniel Judd.

> Years ago I was given a publication that described The Church of Jesus Christ of Latter-day Saints as not only a non-Christian religion, but also as a "cult." The author of the pamphlet, Walter Martin, provided a list of what he termed as the "characteristics of cults" and argued that Latter-day Saints fit his criteria. The Church of Jesus Christ of Latter-day Saints appears to fit the author's criteria for a "cult," but ironically, so does . . . the church Jesus established when He was upon the earth. The following list contains Walter Martin's "characteristics of cults," and a description of how The Church of Jesus Christ of Latter-day Saints and the Church in the days of Jesus both fit the criteria:
>
> "Cults are usually started by strong and dynamic leaders." Joseph Smith, Jr., was indeed a strong and dynamic leader, as was Peter, Paul, and, above all else, the Savior Himself.

"All cults possess some scripture that is either added to or which replaces the Bible." The Book of Mormon is additional scripture, but so were the New Testament Epistles considered "additions" to the Hebrew Bible.

"Rigid standards for membership." Latter-day Saints are invited to not smoke tobacco or drink alcohol and are asked to pay a 10-percent tithe, etc., Jesus taught, "Ye have heard that it was said by them of old time, Thou shalt not commit adultery: But I say unto you, That whosoever looketh on a woman to lust after her hath committed adultery with her already in his heart." (Matthew 5:27–28). Jesus invited His followers to live by a higher law.

"Cultists often become members of one cult after membership in one or more other cults." Many members of the LDS Church are converts to the Church of Jesus Christ, just as some of John the Baptist's former followers were converts in the Savior's day (See John 1:35–37).

"Spend much of their time evangelizing new converts." The LDS Church has several hundred thousand converts each year and maintains a force of 60,000 young missionaries serving in 333 missions throughout the world. Jesus taught the disciples of His day, "Go ye therefore, and teach all nations, baptizing them in the name of the Father, and of the Son, and of the Holy Ghost." (Matthew 28:19–20)

"Leaders . . . are not professional clergymen." The LDS Church does not have an academically trained clergy—they have a lay leadership. The early apostles Peter and John, "were unlearned and ignorant men." (Acts 4:13) Peter, James, and John were fishermen. Jesus was a carpenter.

"A system of doctrine and practice which is in some state of flux." The LDS Church formally discontinued the practice of plural marriage in 1890. During the time of Jesus, the gospel was taught only to Israelites (see Matthew 15:22–24). After Jesus had been crucified, the policy changed when Peter was given the revelation from God to take the gospel to the Gentiles (see Acts chapter 10).

"All cults believe that there is continual . . . communication from God." Latter-day Saints do believe that God continues to communicate to His children today. God has always communicated His will through His prophets (see Amos 3:7, Numbers 12:6, and Acts 10).

"Cults claim to have truth not available to any other groups or individuals." The LDS Church teaches that it is the Lord's authorized church, but membership is available to anyone who is willing to genuinely accept the invitation to follow Jesus Christ. Jesus taught, "I am the way, the truth, and the life: no man cometh unto the Father, but by me" (John 14:6). The Jews saw Jesus as a threat.

"Cultic Vocabulary." As with any organization, the LDS Church has a vocabulary that is unique, i.e., stake centers (churches), MTC (Missionary Training Center), baptism for the dead, etc. First century Christianity introduced such terms as Millennium, Second Coming, baptism, Holy Ghost, etc. Any organization, true or untrue, will possess a distinctive vocabulary.

I concluded our conversation by testifying to Tory, "The Church of Jesus Christ of Latter-day Saints is the kingdom of God on earth. Others may speak evil of that which is good and dogs may bark at the wheels of the chariot, but the caravan moves on."

30

Who will accept our message?

An institute student of mine had been dating a young woman not of our faith. Her uncle is a fifth generation Latter-day Saint who apostatized and joined Calvary Baptist Church. He fed his family and relatives with volumes of material critical of the Church. My student had developed strong feelings for this young lady and called to inquire if I would answer some of her questions. She e-mailed me forty-five pages containing twenty-seven questions. It was apparent that these were not her thoughts but were the result of downloading anti-Mormon literature.

I convinced them to attend my evening Book of Mormon class after which I answered her questions for an hour and a half. Her body language showed resistance and hostility toward me. Our discussion ended by reading John 9 together.

> And as Jesus passed by, he saw a man which was blind from his birth.
>
> And his disciples asked him, saying, Master, who did sin, this man, or his parents, that he was born blind?
>
> Jesus answered, Neither hath this man sinned, nor his parents: but that the works of God should be made manifest in him. . . .
>
> When he had thus spoken, he spat on the ground, and made clay of the spittle, and he anointed the eyes of the blind man with the clay,
>
> And said unto him, Go, wash in the pool of Siloam, (which is by interpretation, Sent.) He went his way therefore, and washed, and came seeing. . . .
>
> . . . Then again the Pharisees also asked him how he had received his sight. He said unto them, He put clay upon mine eyes, and I washed, and do see.
>
> Therefore said some of the Pharisees, This man is not of God, because he keepeth not the sabbath day. Others said, How can a man that is a sinner do such miracles? And there was a division among them.
>
> They say unto the blind man again, What sayest thou of him, that he hath opened thine eyes? He said, He is a prophet.

But the Jews did not believe concerning him, that he had been blind, and received his sight, until they called the parents of him that had received his sight.

And they asked them, saying, Is this your son, who ye say was born blind? how then doth he now see?

His parents answered them and said, We know that this is our son, and that he was born blind:

But by what means he now seeth, we know not; or who hath opened his eyes, we know not: he is of age; ask him: he shall speak for himself. . . .

. . . Then again called they the man that was blind, and said unto him, Give God the praise: we know that this man is a sinner.

He answered and said, Whether he be a sinner or no, I know not: one thing I know, that, whereas I was blind, now I see.

Then said they to him again, What did he to thee? how opened he thine eyes?

He answered them, I have told you already, and ye did not hear: wherefore would ye hear it again? will ye also be his disciples?

Then they reviled him, and said, Thou art his disciple; but we are Moses' disciples.

We know that God spake unto Moses: as for this fellow, we know not from whence he is."

I explained to this inquiring couple, "Jesus, on the Sabbath day, healed a man born blind. The Jews accused Christ of a Sabbath day violation and called him a sinner, disregarding Him and His miracle. These Jews had eyes to see but were spiritually blind and rejected the Savior. The irony is that the man born blind could see that Jesus was the promised Messiah and worshipped him."

Elder Bruce R. McConkie said:

Who will believe our words, and who will hear our message? Who will honor the name of Joseph Smith and accept the gospel restored through his instrumentality?

We answer: the same people who would have believed the words of the Lord Jesus and the ancient Apostles and prophets had they lived in their day.

If you believe the words of Joseph Smith, you would have believed what Jesus and the ancients said.

If you reject Joseph Smith and his message, you would have rejected Peter and Paul and their message...

We testify that God has given to us his everlasting gospel, and we invite all men to come and partake of its blessings with us."[83]

I asked my student and his girlfriend if he they had lived two thousand years ago, could they accept Christ and reject Peter and Paul? They were reflective for a moment and then admitted, "No, I guess not."

I told them, "After the ascension of Christ into heaven, Peter was the president of the Church. He held the keys of the kingdom (see Matthew 16:19). He received his authority from Jesus Christ Himself (see Mark 3:14–15). By revelation, Paul was called to be an apostle and was ordained by the apostles before he preached the gospel and administered in the ordinances thereof (see Acts 13:2–3). Both Peter and Paul were eyewitnesses of the resurrected Christ (see 1 Corinthians 15:5–8). Peter wrote two books, and Paul wrote fourteen books in the New Testament. As the authorized servants of the Savior, they directed the affairs of Christ's church.

"Likewise, Joseph Smith was called of God and was an eyewitness of the resurrected Christ. He, too, received the keys of the priesthood under the hands of those who held it anciently, administered the ordinances of the gospel, directed the affairs of the restored church, and brought forth additional scripture. Just as we could not fully accept Christ and reject the divinely chosen authorized apostles Peter and Paul in former times, we cannot fully accept Christ and reject the divinely chosen, authorized Prophet Joseph Smith in latter days."

There was a long silence. I invited the young lady to continue to investigate our message of truth and salvation. She agreed to do so with an open mind.

---

83. Bruce R. McConkie, in Conference Report, October 1981, 69; or *Ensign*, November 1981, 48.

31

The Book of Mormon is an addition to the Bible. Therefore, you are accursed!

Revelation 22:18–19 states, "For I testify unto every man that heareth the words of the prophecy of this book, If any man shall add unto these things, God shall add unto him the plagues that are written in this book: And if any man shall take away from the words of the book of this prophecy, God shall take away his part out of the book of life, and out of the holy city, and *from* the things which are written in this book."

I have been told too many times to count, "The Book of Mormon is an addition to the Bible. Therefore, you are accursed!" The word *Bible* is of Greek origin, being derived from *ta biblia*, "the books." According to author James L. Barker, "When the books of the New Testament were written, there was no copyright. In consequence John warns against changing his text of The Revelation."[84]

Elder Jeffrey R. Holland explained, "There is now overwhelming consensus among virtually all biblical scholars that this verse applies only to the book of Revelation, *not* the whole Bible. Those scholars of our day acknowledge a number of New Testament 'books' that were almost certainly written *after* John's revelation on the Isle of Patmos were received. Included in this category are at least the books of Jude, the three Epistles of John, and probably the entire Gospel of John itself. Perhaps there are even more than these."[85]

Moses made a similar admonition to John's prohibiting the alteration of his books of scripture: "Ye shall not add unto the word which I command you, neither shall ye diminish ought from it, that ye may keep the commandments of the Lord your God which I command you" (Deuteronomy 4:2).

If you apply your interpretation of Revelation 22:18–19 to Moses's admonition in Deuteronomy 4:2, then every prophet from Joshua, Isaiah, Jeremiah, Ezekiel, along with John, Jude, and the apostles in the New Testament are all accursed.

---

84. James L. Barker, *Apostasy from the Divine Church*, 14–15.
85. Jeffrey R. Holland, in Conference Report, April 2008.

32

The Bible is scripture that teaches Christian principles. What is the purpose of the Book of Mormon?

On a number of occasions, I have been invited to private Catholic schools to explain our beliefs and answer their questions. On a few of these visits a student commented, "The Bible is scripture that teaches Christian principles. What is the purpose of the Book of Mormon?"

I answered, "So that we understand each other, let me ask you two questions. Do you believe the following are Christian principles? 'Believe in the Son of God, that He came to redeem His people and suffered and died to atone for their sins; and that He rose again from the dead, which brought to pass the Resurrection, that all men shall stand before Him to be judged.'"

They always answer with a resounding "Yes!"

I continue, "My second question is, do you believe this verse is scripture? 'There shall be no other name given nor any other way nor means whereby salvation can come unto the children of men, only in and through the name of Christ, the Lord Omnipotent.'"

Again, they respond in the affirmative. "Of course, salvation comes only through Jesus Christ!" They are shocked when I inform them that I just shared two of the 6,607 verses in the Book of Mormon: Alma 33:22 and Mosiah 3:17. I remind them, "You just agreed that the Book of Mormon is scripture that teaches Christian principles."

Then I say, "As to the second part of your question, 'What is the purpose of the Book of Mormon,' I will give three important purposes for the book in 1 Nephi 13:40. 'These last records, which thou hast seen among the Gentiles, shall establish the truth of the first, which are of the twelve apostles of the Lamb, and shall make known the plain and precious things which have been taken away from them; and shall make known to all kindreds, tongues, and people, that the Lamb of God is the Son of the Eternal Father, and the Savior of the world; and that all men must come unto him, or they cannot be saved.' The Book of Mormon establishes the truth of the Bible, makes known the plain and precious things that have been removed from the Bible, and is another testament of Jesus Christ (see 2 Corinthians 13:1)."

Inevitably the class asks, "What are the plain and precious things that have been taken from the Bible?"

The students are astounded when I apprise them of the ensuing facts. I teach them, "The doctrine of Christ as it pertains to what we need to do to be saved consist of five things: faith, repentance, baptism, receiving the gift of the Holy Ghost, and enduring to the end. Notice the difference between the Old Testament and the Book of Mormon during the exact same time period."

DOCTRINE	TIMES WE SEE THE WORD IN THE OLD TESTAMENT	TIMES IT APPEARS IN THE BC PORTION OF THE BOOK OF MORMON (1 NEPHI– HELAMAN, ETHER)
Faith	2	200
Repentance	1	265
Baptism	0	68
Holy Ghost	0	35
Endure to the End	0	7

LOST BOOKS

The Bible Dictionary states:

The so-called lost books of the Bible are those documents that are mentioned in the Bible in such a way that it is evident they were considered authentic and valuable, but that are not found in the Bible today. Sometimes called missing scripture, they consist of at least the following: book of the Wars of the Lord (Num. 21:14); book of Jasher (Josh. 10:13; 2 Sam. 1:18); book of the acts of Solomon (1 Kings 11:42); book of Samuel the seer (1 Chronicles 29: 29); . . . book of Gad the seer (1 Chronicles 29:29); book of Nathan the prophet (1 Chronicles 29:29; 2 Chronicles 9:29); prophecy of Ahijah (2 Chronicles 9:29); visions of Iddo the seer (2 Chronicles 9:29); 12:15; 13:22); book of Shemaiah (2 Chronicles

12:15); book of Jehu (2 Chronicles 20:34); sayings of the seers (2 Chronicles 33:19); an epistle of Paul to the Corinthians, earlier than our present 1 Corinthians (1 Corinthians 5:9); possibly an earlier epistle to the Ephesians (Ephesians 3:3); an epistle to the Church at Laodicea (Colossians 4:16); and some prophecies of Enoch, known to Jude (Jude 1:14). (Bible Dictionary, 725–726).

I invite the class to read Paul's writings in Colossians 4:16: "And when this epistle is read among you, cause that it be read also in the church of the Laodiceans; and that ye likewise read the epistle from Laodicea."

I ask the students. "The apostle Paul requested that we read the epistle from Laodicea. Please turn in your Bible to the book of Laodiceans." It is interesting to watch as they frantically look through their scriptures to find this epistle without success. After a while they look up at me with a puzzled expression on their faces.

I apprise them that Bible scholar Scott R. Petersen's research reveals, "There are more than eight thousand manuscript copies of the New Testament, 5,366 alone in the Greek language—yet no two of them are identical. The oldest surviving manuscript copy is from the late second century, at which point the theological controversies had been raging for at least one hundred years. "All existing manuscripts have been copied numerous times—'copies of copies of copies'; there are no extant original autographs. In fact, most manuscripts come from the eighth and ninth centuries with prized copies coming from the fourth century. Scholars admit that no one knows how many variations exist, but they doubtless number in the hundreds of thousands."[86]

I finish my answer by stating, "So there you have it. There are many plain and precious truths that are no longer found in the Bible. Hence, you can plainly see the purpose and importance of the Book of Mormon."

---

86. Scott R. Petersen, *Where Have All the Prophets Gone?*, 176.

33

"My father taught that missionary work brings a remission of sins"

Brent Dyer and I served concurrently as bishops in San Clemente, California. He is the son of Elder Alvin R. Dyer, who served in the First Presidency with David O. McKay. At a bishop's training meeting with the stake presidency, Bishop Dyer said, "My father taught that missionary work brings a remission of sins."

I responded, "That's scriptural."

He and the other bishops said, "Where is that found in the scriptures?"

I quoted James 5:19–20: "Brethren, if any of you do err from the truth, and one convert him; Let him know, that he which converteth the sinner from the error of his way shall save a soul from death, and shall hide a multitude of sins." I explained that the Lord is so appreciative when we bring his lost sheep back into the fold and "save a soul from death" that He rewards us by hiding a multitude of our sins. I then recited Doctrine and Covenants 31:5: "Therefore, thrust in your sickle with all your soul, and your sins are forgiven you."

There are many blessings in addition to forgiveness for sins when we are actively engaged in bringing souls to Christ. When teaching this principle, I share the following statements from President Hinckley:

> I promise you that the time you spend in the mission field, if those years are spent in dedicated service, will yield a greater return on investment than any other two years of your lives. You will come to know what dedication and consecration mean. You will develop powers of persuasion which will bless your entire life. Your timidity, your fears, your shyness will gradually disappear as you go forth with boldness and conviction. You will learn to work with others, to develop a spirit of teamwork. The cankering evil of selfishness will be supplanted by a sense of service to others. You will draw nearer to the Lord than you likely will in any other set of circumstances. You will come to know that without His help you are indeed weak and simple, but that with His help you can accomplish miracles.

You will establish habits of industry. You will develop a talent for the establishment of goals of effort. You will learn to work with singleness of purpose. What a tremendous foundation all of this will become for you in your later educational efforts and your life's work.[87]

If you serve a mission faithfully and well, you will be a better husband, you will be a better father, you will be a better student, a better worker in your chosen vocation. Love is of the essence of this missionary work. Selflessness is of its very nature. Self-discipline is its requirement. Prayer opens its reservoir of power.[88]

President Gordon B. Hinckley further taught that every missionary should come home with these 10 assets:

A knowledge of and love for God our Eternal Father and His Beloved Son, the Lord Jesus Christ.
A knowledge of and love for the scriptures, the word of the Lord.
An increased love for parents.
A love for the people among whom they labor.
An appreciation for hard work.
The assurance that the inspiration of the Holy Spirit is available to each of us when we live for it.
An understanding of the importance of teamwork.
The value of personal virtue.
The faith to act.
The humility to pray.[89]

Elder Richard G. Scott acknowledged the eternal impact that a mission had on his life: "All that I now hold dear in life began to mature in the mission field. Had I not been encouraged to be a missionary I would not have the eternal companion or precious family I dearly love. I am confident that I would not have had the exceptional professional opportunities that stretched my every capacity. I am certain that I would not have received the sacred callings with

87. Gordon B. Hinckley, "Of Missions, Temples, and Stewardship," *Ensign*, November 1995, 51–52.
88. Hinckley, *Teachings of Gordon B. Hinckley*, 356.
89. Hinckley, "The Message: Gifts to Bring Home from the Mission Field," *New Era*, March 2007, 2–4.

opportunities to serve for which I will be eternally grateful. My life has been richly blessed beyond measure because I served a mission."[90]

The *Church News* researched and published the activity of returned missionaries, which reveals that for the most part, they remain true and faithful in the Church throughout their lives.

85%—Hold a current temple recommend
75%—Study the scriptures at least once a week
71%—Have a personal prayer at least once a day
91%—Attend sacrament meeting at least 3 times a month
92%—Pay a full tithe
97%—Observe the word of wisdom
89%—Hold at least one church position
95%—Married in the temple[91]

The blessings that come to those who serve an honorable mission are profound and limitless.

---

90. Elder Richard G. Scott, "Now Is the Time to Serve," in Conference Report, April 2006, 93)
91. *Church News*, 14 June 1980.

34

"Tell her you're a member of the Church!"

One summer I became very sick with mononucleosis, measles, and strep throat. A family in my ward took me into their home and nursed me back to health. When I began to feel better, their seven-year-old daughter asked me to hit some tennis balls with her in the street. After we had done this for a while, I noticed their neighbor came outside to work in her front yard. I said to Tiffany, "Go tell her you're a member of the Church."

This bold little seven-year-old approached her neighbor and said, "Have you seen my CTR ring?"

The neighbor said, "No, what does CTR mean?"

Tiffany said, "Choose the right when a choice is placed before you."

"Where did you get it?"

"In Primary.

"What's Primary?"

"It's an organization for little kids under twelve."

"What do you do in Primary?"

"We learn about Jesus and the gospel. We're taught to be honest and obey our parents."

"Is that a church organization?"

"Yes."

"What church do you go to?"

"The Church of Jesus Christ of Latter-day Saints! It's the true church!"

I know the Lord was well pleased with Tiffany for sharing the gospel with her neighbor in such a beautiful and childlike manner. "It becometh every man who hath been warned to warn his neighbor" (D&C 88:81).

35

If I knew there is a living prophet on the earth today, no storm, barking dog, amount of rejection, or sacrifice could deter me from declaring our message

Before the Missionary Training Center was constructed in Provo, Utah, missionaries reported to the Salt Lake City Mission Home to begin their missions. When I was there, our mission president informed us that on the following day we would do an endowment session in the Salt Lake Temple. Afterward, President Harold B. Lee would address us for an hour and a half to answer any questions we had about the Church, our doctrine, or the temple.

I immediately began to fast and pray, and to prepare myself spiritually for this once-in-a-lifetime experience. That night I knelt by my bedside for at least twenty minutes, and I asked the Lord that the Spirit would bear witness to me of the divine calling of Harold B. Lee. I knew that Jesus is the Christ, Joseph Smith is a prophet, that the Church is true, and that the Book of Mormon is the word of God. Nevertheless, I couldn't honestly say that I knew through the power of the Holy Ghost that Harold B. Lee was a living prophet. It was Harold B. Lee himself who said, "That person is not truly converted until he sees the power of God resting upon the leaders of this Church, and until it goes down into his heart like fire."[92]

I realized that if I had this witness, I would work harder, teach with power and authority, testify with greater conviction, and serve a better mission. If I knew there is a prophet in the land who can authoritatively say, "Thus saith the Lord and it shall surely come to pass," no storm, barking dog, amount of rejection, or sacrifice could detour me from declaring our message of the restored gospel.

After my prayer, I got into bed and continued in prayer through the remainder of the night. I had never before prayed all night for a

---

92. Harold B. Lee, "The Strength of the Priesthood," *Ensign*, July 1972, 103.

particular blessing. I pleaded earnestly with the Lord that I would receive this affirmation.

The following day after completing the endowment session, the temple workers directed us upstairs to the assembly room. There were 396 missionaries in our group. I was about half of the way back from the front of the line. The first missionaries to enter the room were directed to the rows on the left half of the room. As I entered the assembly room, a temple worker stopped me momentarily and then directed me to the front row, front seat, on the right side.

In honor of the prophet, we rose to our feet when President Lee entered the room. He came from the back of the room and moved forward. He walked down the aisle and across the front row of missionaries, right up to me, and shook my hand. We visited for a moment. He asked my name, where I was from, and where I was called to serve. When I mentioned the Montana–Wyoming Mission, he informed me that he had served in the Central States Mission. He assured me that I would love the good-hearted people in that region of the country and enjoy great success. I was amazed that he singled me out of this entire group. As we talked, my heart burned within me. Now, I know the difference between excitement and heartburn. This was different. I had a warm, peaceful assurance that Harold B. Lee was a prophet of God. As he spoke from the pulpit, he occasionally looked in my eyes and directed his remarks specifically to me. I felt a burning in my bosom, which reoccurred again and again.

Following his remarks, the first question someone asked the prophet was, "Where in the temple did the Lord appear to Lorenzo Snow?" At the death of President Woodruff, Lorenzo Snow, senior member of the twelve apostles and next in succession to become the prophet, retired to the sacred altar of the temple. He poured out his heart in prayer for guidance and inspiration for his new calling. The account informs us that after finishing his prayer he expected a reply, some special manifestation from the Lord. So he waited . . . and waited . . . and waited. There was no reply, no voice, no visitation, no manifestation. He left the altar and the room in great disappointment. Passing through the celestial room and out into the large corridor, a glorious manifestation was given President Snow, which I relate in the words of his granddaughter, Allie Young Pond:

> One evening while I was visiting Grandpa Snow in his room in the Salt Lake Temple, I remained until the door keepers had gone and the night-watchmen had not yet come in, so grandpa said he would

take me to the main front entrance and let me out that way. He got his bunch of keys from his dresser. After we left his room, and while we were still in the large corridor leading into the celestial room, I was walking several steps ahead of grandpa when he stopped and said, "Wait a moment, Allie, I want to tell you something. It was right here that the Lord Jesus Christ appeared to me at the time of the death of President Woodruff. He instructed me to go right ahead and reorganize the First Presidency of the Church at once and not wait as had been done after the death of the previous presidents, and that I was to succeed President Woodruff."

Then grandpa came a step nearer and held out his left hand and said, "He stood right here, about three feet above the floor. It looked as though he stood on a plate of solid gold."

Grandpa told me what a glorious personage the Savior is and described his hands, feet, countenance and beautiful white robes, all of which were of such glory of whiteness and brightness that he could hardly gaze upon him.

Then he came another step nearer and put his right hand on my head and said: "Now granddaughter, I want you to remember that this is the testimony of your grandfather, that he told you with his own lips that he actually saw the Savior, here in the temple, and talked with him face to face."[93]

President Lee confirmed, "Jesus Christ is closer to this Church and appears more often in holy places than any of us realize, except those to whom he makes personal appearances. We hesitate to refer to any particular place, because just as you walk the hallways of your home, the Lord walks the corridors of His temple." Then he added, "Where else would the Lord be when He visits the earth than in His own house?"

When I left the temple that day, I knew there was a living prophet of God on the earth, and that the temple is His holy house. I am so grateful for this experience. Knowing what I then knew, my desire and capacity to serve the Lord, proclaim His gospel, and build His kingdom was strengthened. If we hunger and thirst after righteousness, we will be filled with the Holy Ghost and receive an answer to our prayers.

---

93. LeRoi C. Snow, "An Experience of My Father's," *Improvement Era*, September 1933, Vol. 36:677.

36

The conversion of the Prince of Chad could impact his entire nation

For three years I was privileged to serve in the California Carlsbad Mission presidency with Merlyn K. Jolley. President Jolley served faithfully in the Church as a bishop, high councilman, and member of the Garden Grove, California, stake presidency. After a distinguished career with AT&T, the Jolleys retired and moved into their dream home in South Jordan, Utah. When their home was completed and the landscaping was finished, the Jolleys found they had a lot of spare time on their hands. After a dedicated lifetime of work and church service, the Jolleys felt they could do something better than sit around watching *The Price Is Right* on TV in their golden years. They decided to volunteer as Temple Square missionaries at the Salt Lake City visitors center.

One day the Prince of Chad, Africa, came with an entourage of six others to Temple Square. Merlyn Jolley was assigned to give them a three-hour tour, which included the outside of the temple, the museum, the assembly hall, a concert in the Tabernacle, and the visitors center. The tour concluded at the base of the Christus statue, where Merlyn Jolley bore testimony of the Savior Jesus Christ and His restored gospel.

The Prince of Chad said, "What is required to join your church?"

President Jolley replied, "It's not that easy. You need to take the missionary lessons, understand the principles of the gospel, and be committed to living them the remainder of your life."

The prince then inquired, "How long does that take?"

Brother Jolley answered, "At least a week."

The prince told his aide, "Make arrangements for us to stay in Salt Lake City for a week."

A sister missionary at Temple Square from Africa who spoke his language gave him the lessons. At the end of the week, the Prince of Chad was baptized in the Tabernacle basement.

When President Jolley told me this story, I likened it to the conversion of King Lamoni (see Alma 18–19). Brother Jolley said to me, "President Greiner, this was no big deal. I just gave a tour. Anyone could have done it."

I countered, "You were in the right place, at the right time, with the right spirit which resulted in the conversion of the Prince of Chad into The Church of Jesus Christ of Latter-day Saints, which will greatly impact his entire country!"

After several attempts I persuaded President Jolley to call Church Headquarters and get an update on the Prince of Chad. President Jolley learned that after the prince returned to his homeland, he wrote to the Church, saying, "My father the king has agreed to donate land if you would like to build a church here." They seized the moment and constructed a chapel in Chad.

President Jolley also learned that a year after the prince's baptism, he returned to Salt Lake City, was ordained an elder, endowed, and sealed to his family in the temple.

Merlyn K. Jolley was the Lord's instrument to bring about the Prince of Chad's miraculous conversion, which may result in numerous baptisms because he had a desire to serve God and was called to the work (see D&C 4:3).

37

The Spirit said, "Slow down!"

Nephi told his brothers, "Ye have heard his voice from time to time; and he hath spoken unto you in a still small voice" (1 Nephi 17:45). Helaman explained, "It was a still voice of perfect mildness. As if it had been a whisper, and it did pierce even unto the soul" (Helaman 5:30). Let me relate an experience when the still small voice saved my life.

After training a new district leader of his responsibilities, my companion and I were traveling to Worland, Wyoming, to spend the night. Since there were no speed limit laws at that time in the states of Montana and Wyoming, I was driving about eighty-five miles per hour. We had just passed a big semi-diesel truck, and we were approaching the Wind River Canyon, when the Spirit said, "Slow down!"

I turned to my companion and said, "I better slow down."

Elder Godfrey responded, "I don't care. Suit yourself."

It was then that I knew he didn't say, "Slow down." As I pondered this, I realized I heard the words in my mind, not with my ears. Accordingly, I took my foot off the accelerator and slowed down to about sixty. We traveled through three tunnels, leading into the canyon. The Wind River Canyon has a canyon wall about one hundred and fifty feet straight up from the highway. The Wind River is fifty to seventy feet vertically below the road on the other side. As we passed through the third tunnel, we hit black ice. The car began to swerve out of control. My companion said, "Take your foot off the brake." I did. I also took my hands off the steering wheel because it was spinning so fast. We were totally at the Lord's mercy. The car would swerve from one side of the road to the other, and then spin complete circles as we slid over one hundred yards down the street. At one point, we closed our eyes and braced ourselves in anticipation of a crash into the side of the mountain, but it didn't happen. The car spun around again and crossed to the other side of the highway. Here we found ourselves going sixty miles per hour, with the car in drive, going backwards, and looking forward out the windshield. We were about two feet from the edge of the cliff, and there was no guardrail. If we had gone off the cliff at this angle, we would have rolled the car into the river, and we probably would have had no chance for survival. I felt impressed to slam the brakes. The car pivoted on its rear wheels and went off the cliff perpendicular to the highway and into the river about fifty feet below.

The feeling was quite different from the roller coaster ride at Disneyland. It was like going backwards off a five-story building, sixty miles an hour, into a raging river. As we were going off the cliff, I said to Elder Godfrey, "Get out as fast as you can!" I had one hand on the steering wheel and the other on my seat belt. As we hit the water, I threw off my seat belt, opened the door, and stepped into the river. I looked over my shoulder to make sure my companion was not injured. He was fine, so I swam to shore. From the rocks I cheered on my companion. The release button on Elder Godfrey's seat belt was broken. I should mention that our car was a Ford Pinto. It was a real death trap. The only thing this car lacked were handles on the side for the pall-bearers to carry it. Unfortunately, Elder Godfrey was unable to release his seat belt. In desperation he opened the door but with a shoulder strap and seat belt on, he couldn't get out of the car. The force of the river pinned the car door against his right leg. His side of the car began sinking first. The water filled up to the knot on his tie. Now, when you're a traveling Elder, everything you own is in your vehicle: our suits, clothes, Kleenex boxes, scriptures, journals, cameras, maps, Dear John letters, and so on. Elder Godfrey reached through the water and debris and finally disconnected his seat belt. He got out of the car on my side and swam to shore. We began scrambling up the rocks to the highway. After we climbed up to the road, we looked down and observed that our car was completely immersed in the river. To my knowledge it was the first Ford Pinto baptized by authority in this dispensation.

The semi-diesel, which we had passed, slowed to a stop. He had seen us swerve down the street, rip out sagebrush on the side of the road, and drive off the cliff. Furthermore, I had forgotten to turn off the car's headlights, which shone through the water and illuminated the canyon wall. It was beautiful. The truck driver rolled down his window and said, "Wow!"

I said to him, "We're missionaries from The Church of Jesus Christ of Latter-day Saints. What do you know about the Church?"

His reply was, "You guys never quit, do ya?"

The following day, the deputy sheriff in Thermopolis, Wyoming, drove us back to the scene of the accident to tow our car out of the river. As he examined the police records, he informed us that we were the first ones to live through that experience of driving off the road into the Wind River. I believe we're here today to share this story, because a still small voice said, "Slow down!" President Ezra Taft Benson expressed, "The Spirit is the most important matter in this glorious work."[94]

---

94. Ezra Taft Benson, Mission Presidents Seminar, June 21, 1975.

38

Have you heard of the Word of Wisdom?

In Glasgow, Montana, we were working with a part-member family. The mother and her daughter were members of the Church. The father and his three sons were not members. They also had two little boys under the age of eight who really looked up to the missionaries as little children do. One night when we went over to teach the family, we noticed that the little boys had drawn black ties on their white T-shirts with a permanent marker. They were also wearing name tags. One name tag read Elder Carlson, and the really cute boy had a name tag that said Elder Greiner.

Before we started our lesson that night, the boys ran up to me and began swinging from my extended arms. Then they said, "Elder Greiner, you're really strong." I quickly agreed. They challenged me to arm wrestle them. Together we went over to the kitchen table.

After a little struggle, I managed to pin each of them. They said, "Now we know you're really strong." I tried to remain humble and nodded in the affirmative. They said, "We'd like you to arm wrestle our big brother Juney."

I didn't want to arm wrestle Juney. He was about twenty-one, weighed one hundred and ninety pounds, was six-foot-two, and tough as nails. Of course, I didn't want to lose face either, so we began gathering up our materials to go home. I said, "I'd love to arm wrestle him, boys, but we have places to go, people to see, truths to teach, testimonies to bear, souls to save, things to do, and no more time for games."

As we arose to leave their home, lo and behold, Juney showed up. He threw open the door, which crashed into the living room wall, stepped inside, and said, "Howdy."

Juney was a cowboy. He was out wrestling doggies, baling hay, eating beans, and walking in manure all day. The only exercise I got as a missionary was turning the pages of the scriptures and walking door to door. Juney was just bigger and stronger than me. I really didn't care to be humiliated in an arm wrestling match with him. The boys insisted and got the contest underway. I shook Juney's hand and grabbed him by the tips of the fingers and squeezed them together as hard as I could. When he withdrew his hand it resembled a gardening tool. I wanted him to think I was tough. He punched me in the stomach to show me he was tougher. We went over to the kitchen table and began our contest.

We were straining, struggling, and grunting for fifteen minutes. You have no idea as to the amount of pain involved. I had a cramp in my right wrist that spread down my arm, shoulder, and side. It continued all the way to my right foot. I felt paralyzed on that side of my body. Juney was moaning, and great drops of sweat were pouring off his face onto the table. I tried to use a psychological technique and just look into his eyes with a big smile, although I was dying inside. After our excruciating match had continued for what seemed endless, Juney began to pin me, and I was about four inches from defeat. My strength was entirely gone. I looked up at the two little boys with the permanent marker ties and name tags and the family we were trying to unite in the Church, and thought, "I've got to win this thing!" In my moment of desperation a Bible story when Samson lost his strength entered my mind: "And Samson called unto the Lord, and said, O Lord God, remember me, I pray thee, and strengthen me only this once" (Judges 16:28). I began to pray silently. Then I thought to myself, what would Jesus do? Of course, Jesus always taught. So, I inquired of Juney, "Have you heard of the Word of Wisdom?"

Juney answered, "Nope, I've never been too bright."

I explained this is a revelation that Joseph Smith received in 1833. It instructs members of the Church to refrain from coffee, tea, tobacco, alcohol, and harmful drugs. I asked, "Juney, do you use any of these substances?"

He said, "Yep, I use them all." I had observed a spittoon he used when chewing tobacco in the family room. Unfortunately, he was rarely successful at hitting the target.

I stretched it a little bit, but I thought the Lord would understand at this critical moment. I said, "Juney, if one obeys this commandment strictly as I have, you can call upon the Lord in times of need and have the strength of ten men!"

He responded, "Yeah?"

And I exclaimed, "Yeah!"

With a great surge of energy and force, I threw his arm over and pinned him. His knuckles seemed to almost shatter on the hardwood table. He rolled off his chair onto the floor, wincing in anguish. I arose from my chair and tried to raise both arms over my head in a victory sign. I was unable to move my right arm, so I just lifted my left hand.

I learned a great lesson from this experience. We can share the gospel at any time, in any place, and while engaged in almost any activity, if we will just seize the opportunity.

Elder Dallin H. Oaks said at the October 2001 general conference, "The intensity of our desire to share the gospel is a great indicator of the extent of our personal conversion" ("Sharing the Gospel," *Ensign*, November 2001, 7).

39

"The Spirit directed us to your home!"

My last area in the mission field was Cody, Wyoming. Elder Ormsby and I fasted and prayed fervently that the Lord would lead us to someone He had prepared to receive the gospel. My companion and I left our apartment to begin proselyting and got in our car. I said, "I feel impressed we should walk rather than drive."

After walking a considerable distance, we felt inspired to approach a green apartment complex. We knocked on a specific door. A woman named Rosie Wood answered. After we introduced ourselves, she said, "No thanks" and began to close the door.

I knew and had experienced the manifestations of the Spirit and couldn't believe her response. My companion exclaimed, "Wait! We asked the Lord this morning to direct us to a pure in heart person who would listen to our message. The Spirit directed us to your home!"

Immediately she burst into tears. She told us that she had spent the weekend in Casper, Wyoming, with her friend who had just been baptized into the Church. Her acquaintance shared with Rosey her conversion experience and the blessings that the gospel brought into her life. Rosie invited us in, and we gave her the first discussion. We returned that evening and taught her husband and children, Samantha (Sam) and Larry Jr. (Moose). They were very receptive and were subsequently baptized because they had been prepared to receive our message of truth.

We are instructed to "bring to pass the gathering of mine elect; for mine elect hear my voice and harden not their hearts" (D&C 29:7). We felt like Nephi, who taught, "I was led by the spirit, not knowing beforehand the things which I should do." (1 Nephi 4:6)

On April 6, 2004, twenty-nine years later, I received a telephone call from Samantha. She lives in Highland, Utah. She and her mom wanted to locate the missionary who taught them the gospel. Samantha Wood Callier told me she is a BYU graduate, married in the temple, and active in the Church.

That same night Rosie and Larry Wood called my home. Rosie related that she has served faithfully in the Primary, Young Women, and Relief Society auxiliaries since her conversion. She thanked me for bringing the gospel to her family both here and beyond the veil. Rosie shared that she and her husband had moved to Texas and were ordinance workers in the Houston Temple. As of that date they had submitted the names of 5,398 relatives to have their ordinance work done in the House of the Lord. Rosey and Larry began to cry when I shared with them the Prophet Joseph Smith's testimony concerning the work for the dead: "In the resurrection, those who had been worked for [they will] fall at the feet of those who had done their work, kiss their feet, embrace their knees and manifest the most exquisite gratitude. We do not comprehend what a blessing to them these ordinances are."[95]

Apostle Orson F. Whitney said, "There is no joy that can compare with that of a missionary who has been made the instrument for the salvation of a soul."[96]

---

95. *The Vision of the Degrees of Glory*, Nels B. Lundwall, comp., Independence, MI: Zion's Printing and Publishing, 1945, 141.
96. Orson F. Whitney, *The LDS Speaker's Sourcebook*, 282. See also D&C 18:15–16.

40

"How great shall be your joy!"

Shortly after being called as bishop, I attended general conference in the Salt Lake Tabernacle. Between sessions I heard a young man in the balcony cry out, "Brother Greiner!" He was a former seminary student of mine named Lee Jacobs. He said, "I enjoyed your seminary class, served a mission, and this is my wife whom I recently married in the Provo Temple."

Moments later I felt a tap on my shoulder. The brother behind me introduced himself as the stake president from Butte and asked, "Are you Elder Greiner who served your mission in Montana?"

I replied, "Yes, about twelve years ago. Have we ever met?"

He said, "No, but they still talk about you there." Then he added, "Didn't you baptize Rick Given?"

I answered, "Yes, sir. How do you know that?"

He said, "Well, he is now one of my bishops. You also baptized Marty and David Bird, didn't you?"

I replied, "Yes, we did."

He continued, "Elder Bird was just recently released from serving an honorable mission." He then informed me, "Heather Emery, whom you baptized, married Roger Hinckley, and all five of their children served missions and married in the temple."

As I turned back around, tears streamed down my cheeks. I cannot begin to explain the gratitude I felt for having had the opportunity to serve a mission. The words in D&C 18:15–16 came to my mind: "And if it so be that you should labor all your days in crying repentance unto this people, and bring, save it be one soul unto me, how great shall be your joy with him in the kingdom of my Father! And now, if your joy will be great with one soul that you have brought unto me into the kingdom of my Father, how great will be your joy if you should bring many souls unto me."

41

Immediately following the priesthood blessing he came out of his coma

In the April 2010 general conference, Elder Dallin H. Oaks expressed, "Latter-Day Saints believe in applying the best available scientific knowledge and techniques . . . to restore health. The use of medical science is not at odds with our prayers of faith and our reliance on priesthood blessings." The following experience demonstrates this principle:

While I was serving as bishop in 1992, the day after Thanksgiving, Brent and Henriette Cox were riding bicycles near the mission in San Juan Capistrano, California. Brent felt his chest suddenly tighten, and his lungs began to rage with each breath. Henriette yelled to a bystander that her husband was having a heart attack. The bystander immediately dialed 911. Another bystander, who was an off-duty paramedic, stopped to help. Within minutes the ambulance arrived and rushed him to Mission Hospital. Brent came in suffering an acute heart attack, and within fifteen minutes he experienced a massive cardiac arrest. Daniel Kulick, MD, a cardiologist said, "He basically died in the emergency room. We had to act fast because Brent's odds did not look good."

Brent and Henriette's home teacher, Merrill Weech, came to the hospital and gave Brent a priesthood blessing. Dr. Kulick said, "I know who you are. My daughter goes to a lot of your church activities. If you don't mind, I would like a blessing also."

Dr. Kulick opted to perform an angioplasty on Brent and discovered his right coronary artery was 100 percent blocked. Brent was whisked to a surgery suite, where Drew Morris, MD, performed coronary artery bypass surgery. During the bypass operation, Brent's heart stopped yet again. The staff was able to massage his heart until it began beating on its own. Each time Brent's ailing heart stopped, the cardiac team was able to immediately revive him and bring him back to life. His physicians estimate Brent's heart stopped between eight and ten times during his hospital stay. He contracted a staph infection, pneumonia, blood clots in his lungs, and an extremely high fever. This caused him to go into a coma, and he was placed on life support. To complicate matters further, lightning struck the power grid at Mission Hospital (the same day that lightning struck the Angel Moroni on the San Diego Temple), causing the hospital's power to go out. Consequently, the nurses had to manually perform "hand bagging- pumping" to keep his life support system functioning for a period of time.

Doug Higham and I were summoned to the hospital to give Brent another priesthood blessing. When the anointing was sealed and "amen" was said, Brent, for the first time, opened his eyes and came out of his coma. As promised in the blessing, Brent experienced a complete recovery.

After attending our ward temple preparation class, Brent and Henriette Cox were sealed in the San Diego Temple. For nineteen years Brent remained healthy and vibrant. He was a living, walking, and talking miracle of medical science and the power of the priesthood, working together in perfect harmony, until his passing in 2011.

42

His faith is sufficient to be healed

James 5:14–15 states: "Is any sick among you? let him call for the elders of the church; and let them pray over him, anointing him with oil in the name of the Lord: And the prayer of faith shall save the sick, and the Lord shall raise him up; and if he have committed sins, they shall be forgiven him."

While serving in a Brigham Young University bishopric, our elders quorum president, Paul Manwaring, told me of a severe injury he suffered the previous day. He fractured his ankle bone all the way through while sliding into second base during an intramural softball game. Paul worked at the Missionary Training Center in Provo, Utah, where he supervised other teachers. He asked his instructors if they were continuing to have spiritual experiences after their missions and if they could share them with their Elders. It was then he realized that he hadn't enjoyed any such manifestations since he returned home from Germany. Paul felt prompted to ask me for a priesthood blessing. He said, "Russ, I have been fasting two days for the spiritual gift of faith to be healed. I would appreciate if you would fast and pray for the gift of faith to heal. I want to be made whole if it's God's will!"

I had twenty-four hours to fast, pray, and ascertain the will of the Lord to bless Paul. I had to receive an identifiable answer to prayer. I had to know what the Lord would have me say in the blessing. How would it be to promise Paul an immediate recovery, only to have him remove his cast and collapse from his injury?

The following day I went to the MTC for the blessing. Paul invited two Elders to "witness a miracle!" They were struggling and were contemplating if they should quit their missions. Can you imagine the pressure I felt to give this priesthood blessing? The Spirit was in rich abundance, and I received a clear, peaceful prompting that "Paul's faith is sufficient to be healed." Therefore, I commanded, in the name of Jesus Christ, that he be made whole immediately. Because of the outpouring of the Spirit, we were all moved to tears and the four of us embraced. When I left the room, I felt as if I was walking on air. I knew the Lord ratified that ordinance.

Paul asked his doctor to remove the cast because he had been healed. His doctor refused emphatically, stating that he could be held liable for malpractice if there were complications from removing the cast prematurely. He instructed Paul to wear it for a minimum of six more weeks. Paul was now faced with the difficult decision to either keep the cast on his leg or to remove it himself. He decided to saw it off.

A few days later I saw Paul in the BYU library. He arose and walked toward me without the slightest evidence of a limp. He thanked me for the blessing and said that it felt as good as new.

Fast forward twenty years. I encountered Paul Manwaring at the Los Angeles Temple for a training session as colleagues in the Church Educational System. We reminisced about the special spiritual experience we had enjoyed together. He then shared with me the following:

> Early in the morning on the day of the blessing, I went to the temple, still fasting. I was struggling with trying to discern my own level of faith, if what I was asking was in line with the Lord's will and if my motives were pure. As I sat in the celestial room after an endowment session, I prayed most sincerely about these things. I remember at one point looking up and seeing a young missionary enter the room, and I had a strong impression. The Spirit whispered to me, "Today you will walk as comfortably and easily as that Elder." I felt elated and at the same time a deep sense of humility and gratitude. When I got down to the locker room to change my clothes, I felt that same confirmation a second time. I had confidence as I received a blessing at your hands, because of what the Lord revealed to me earlier. The blessing and the confirmation from the Spirit presented me with the strength to make the difficult decision to remove the cast. I knew how that might appear to others. My choice was to either exercise faith or not to exercise faith in the promise of the Spirit and the words you pronounced in the blessing I chose faith, and the promises were confirmed.

I mentioned to him, "It would have been helpful if you had shared that information with me before I administered to you." Independent of each other, Paul and I received the same inspiration and Paul

Manwaring was healed by the Lord because of his great faith and the power of the priesthood.

Paul runs marathons, plays a variety of sports, and even parachutes out of airplanes without any pain or complications.

The Lord said, "I will show miracles, signs, and wonders, unto all those who believe on my name. And whoso shall ask it in my name in faith, they shall cast out devils; they shall heal the sick; they shall cause the blind to receive their sight, and the deaf to hear, the dumb to speak, and the lame to walk." (D&C 35:8–9)

43

Dinner with a dead guy

Elder Vaughn J. Featherstone said:

> Seeking to walk in the Lord's footsteps recently brought me in
> contact with a young man and his father. The young man and a
> friend were up hiking in the lower foothills near Cody, Wyoming.
> The friend jumped across a high-power line that was down, but
> the young man got tangled in it and was electrocuted. The friend
> turned and ran all the way back down to where the father lived—
> and it wasn't a short distance—and told the father that his son had
> been electrocuted and that he was dead. The father, who was not a
> young man, ran all the way back up, taking about fifteen minutes.
> When he got up to where the boy was lying across the wires, he
> somehow removed the boy from the wires with a board or a large
> branch. Then he picked his son up in his arms and held him, saying,
> "In the name of Jesus Christ and by the power and authority of the
> holy Melchizedek Priesthood, I command you to live." The dead
> boy opened up his eyes in his father's arms and was taken to the
> University of Utah Medical Center, where he recovered.[97]

My last assignment in the mission field was Cody, Wyoming. In
my personal journal on February 23, 1975, I wrote:

> Brother Heiden invited us to dinner. He is the other ward mission
> leader. They related the faith-promoting story of their son. While
> hiking in the hills he grabbed a power line, which was hanging
> over the trail. This sent a 2,700 volt or 84 amp shock through his
> body. He caught on fire. His father got to him and had to put
> out the flames on his smoldering clothes. He then commanded the
> lifeless boy to live. Suddenly his eyes opened. They flew him to Salt
> Lake City and he was administered to by Bishop Featherstone. The
> doctors said that his right arm and left hand must be amputated.
> Yet he was promised that he would be made whole. As the doctors
> began to cut they discovered some living tissue and began to graft

---

97. Vaughn J. Featherstone, "Where Following Him Can Lead Us," *Ensign*,
February 1981, 8.

skin. In fact, they operated on him every other day for two weeks and he's had 22 operations since the accident. Now he's a vibrant, happy young man. This was the first time I had dinner with a dead guy who had been brought back to life. I know that the priesthood is the power of God, given to man, to act in his name for the blessing of his children.

44

Ten reasons I joined The Church of Jesus Christ of Latter-day Saints

#10. Education

We believe "the glory of God is intelligence" (D&C 93:36) and that "whatever principle of intelligence we attained unto in this life, it will rise with us in the resurrection" (D&C 130:18). The Church of Jesus Christ of Latter-day Saints is the only church in the world in which members demonstrate *greater* "faith and participation in religious activity as advanced degrees are obtained."[98]

9. The Word of Wisdom

The Prophet Joseph Smith received a revelation in 1833 for Latter-day Saints to refrain from coffee, tea, tobacco, alcohol, drugs, and other harmful substances, and to maintain a healthy diet. We are taught to treat our body as a temple of God and as a dwelling place for His Spirit. President Gordon B. Hinckley reported, "Dr. James E. Enstrom from the University of California Los Angeles, who is not a member of the Church and speaks with complete objectivity, reported that Latter-day Saints live about ten years longer than their peers."[99]

What would you do for ten more years of life?

8. Youth Programs/Relief Society

In Proverbs 22:6 we read, "Train up a child in the way he should go: and when he is old, he will not depart from it." The Church of Jesus Christ of Latter-day Saints sponsors one of the largest youth

---

98. Gordon B. Hinckley, in Conference Report, October 1997, 94.
99. Gordon B. Hinckley, "Rise Up, O Men of God," in Conference Report, October 2006.

programs in the world. The Young Women theme for girls turning twelve to eighteen states:

I am a beloved daughter of heavenly parents, with a divine nature and eternal destiny.

As a disciple of Jesus Christ, I strive to become like Him. I seek and act upon personal revelation and minister to others in His holy name.

I will stand as a witness of God at all times and in all things and in all places.

As I strive to qualify for exaltation, I cherish the gift of repentance and seek to improve each day. With faith, I will strengthen my home and family, make and keep sacred covenants, and receive the ordinances and blessings of the holy temple.

The Young Men Statement for boys turning twelve to eighteen declares:

I am a beloved son of God, and He has a work for me to do.

With all my heart, might, mind, and strength, I will love God, keep my covenants, and use His priesthood to serve others, beginning in my own home.

As I strive to serve, exercise faith, repent, and improve each day, I will qualify to receive temple blessings and the enduring joy of the gospel.

I will prepare to become a diligent missionary, loyal husband, and loving father by being a true disciple of Jesus Christ.

I will help prepare the world for the Savior's return by inviting all to come unto Christ and receive the blessings of His Atonement.

What parent would not want their daughters or sons to participate in such inspired programs as these?

The Relief Society women's organization is the oldest in the United States and the largest in the world. Its leadership is comprised of women on the local, regional, and international level. The Relief Society theme is "Charity never faileth" (1 Corinthians 13:8). The Relief Society mission statement proclaims: "Relief Society helps prepare women for the blessings of eternal life (see Moses 1:39) as they increase faith in Heavenly Father and Jesus Christ and His Atonement; strengthen individuals, families, and homes through ordinances and covenants; and work in unity to help those in need." Is it any wonder that women are our better half?

7. The Gift of the Holy Ghost

"The special office of the Holy Ghost is to enlighten and ennoble the mind, to purify and sanctify the soul, to incite to good works, and to reveal the things of God."[100]

"[The Holy Ghost] will whisper peace and joy to [your] soul; it will take malice, hatred, strife and all evil from [our] heart; and [your] whole desire will be to do good."[101]

6. Temples

By the authority of the priesthood that binds on earth and seals in heaven (see Matthew 16:19), we are married in our temples for time and all eternity rather than "till death do you part." Among those married in the temple, the divorce rate is significantly lower than the national level. Latter-day Saints believe that families can be together forever. The deepest desire of my heart is for the Greiner family to be a forever family.

5. Living Prophets and Continuing Revelation

The following scriptures teach us about prophets and continuing revelation:

Surely the Lord God will do nothing, but he revealeth his secret unto his servants the prophets. (Amos 3:7)

Search these commandments, for they are true and faithful, and the prophecies and promises which are in them shall all be fulfilled.

---

100. James E. Talmage, *The Articles of Faith*, 167.
101. Joseph Smith, quoted in *Manuscript History of Brigham Young: 1846–47*, Historical Department, The Church of Jesus Christ of Latter-day Saints, 528–31.

What I the Lord have spoken, I have spoken, and I excuse not myself; and though the heavens and the earth pass away, my word shall not pass away, but shall all be fulfilled, whether by mine own voice or by the voice of my servants, it is the same. (D&C 1:37–38)

For his word ye shall receive, as if from mine own mouth, in all patience and faith.

For by doing these things the *gates of hell shall not prevail against you; yea, and the Lord God will disperse the powers of darkness from before you, and cause the heavens to shake for your good, and his name's glory. (D&C 21:5–6)

We believe all that God has revealed, all that He does now reveal, and we believe that He will yet reveal many great and important things pertaining to the Kingdom of God. (Articles of Faith 1:9)

We definitely need His guidance and instruction today in our present circumstances as much as those led anciently by prophets and apostles?

4. The Church of Jesus Christ of Latter-day Saints

I belong to The Church of Jesus Christ of Latter-day Saints. Many churches are named after their location, founders, doctrines, or creeds. But down to the beginning of the nineteenth century, no church on earth was even named the Church of Jesus Christ. Each year hundreds of thousands of converts are baptized into The Church of Jesus Christ of Latter-day Saints from around the world. In November 2000, *US News and World Report* reported The Church of Jesus Christ of Latter-day Saints as the fastest-growing church on the earth.

3. Priesthood Authority

"What is Priesthood? It is the rule and government of God, whether on earth, or in the heavens; and it is the only legitimate power, the only authority that is acknowledged by Him to rule and regulate the affairs of

His Kingdom."[102] We believe that priesthood authority was divinely restored by the angelic messengers John the Baptist, Peter, James, and John to Joseph Smith and Oliver Cowdery in 1829. Every male member of the Church, from the newest twelve–year-old deacon to the President of the Church can trace his priesthood authority back to Jesus Christ. I am honored to serve and bless my family as the patriarch in my home.

2. The Book of Mormon—Another Testament of Jesus Christ

The Book of Mormon has 6,607 verses. Of these, 3,925 refer to Jesus Christ by 101 different titles. On the average, every 1.68 verses mention Christ by name. Whether He is honored as Creator, Prince of Peace, Messiah, Only Begotten Son, Advocate, Mediator, Savior, Author and Finisher of Salvation, or King of Kings, the Book of Mormon testifies that Jesus is the Christ more often than any other book ever written in the history of the world (25 percent more often than the New Testament). My love for the Savior has grown tremendously as I have studied daily from this sacred testament.

1. The First Vision

While praying to know which of all the many different Christian churches he should join, Joseph Smith declared, "I saw a pillar of light exactly over my head, above the brightness of the sun, which descended gradually until it fell upon me. . . . When the light rested upon me I saw two Personages, whose brightness and glory defy all description, standing above me in the air. One of them spake unto me, calling me by name, and said, pointing to the other—'This is My Beloved Son. Hear Him!'" (Joseph Smith—History 1:16–17).

I thank my Father in Heaven for calling a prophet in our day who speaks the mind, will, word, and voice of the Lord and the power of God unto salvation (see Doctrine and Covenants 68:4).

---

102. John Taylor, *Journal of Discourses*, 1:224.

45

If you live it, you'll be happy;
if you don't, you won't

Several months after my conversion, I attended my first general conference of the Church. In the priesthood session I was fortunate to sit by a very valiant stake president. Throughout the meeting he bore witness to me of the truthfulness of the messages and the divine calling of the Brethren. When the session concluded he asked, "Would you like to meet one of the General Authorities?"

I said, "Oh yes, I'd love to!" I was really excited.

We worked our way down from the balcony onto the floor level, where some of the brethren were still mingling with the members. Ezra Taft Benson happened to be free for a moment. This good stake president said, "Elder Benson, I'd like for you to meet a friend of mine. He is a new member of the Church, and I thought you might have some advice for him."

I was very anxious in anticipation of what he might say to me. Here was an Apostle of the Lord like Peter, James, and John, who was going to give me inspired counsel.

Elder Benson shook my hand, looked me in the eye, and said, "If you live it, you'll be happy. If you don't, you won't."

I thought to myself, *What a rip off!* I was expecting a personal prophetic epistle or something profound like Doctrine and Covenants 19 to Martin Harris.

As I have reflected upon Elder Benson's statement to me, I have come to realize that it is very profound and is absolutely, positively true! Joseph Smith said, "Happiness is the object and design of our existence; and will be the end thereof, if we pursue the path that leads to it; and this path is virtue, uprightness, faithfulness, holiness, and keeping all the commandments of God."[103]

King Benjamin testified, "And moreover, I would desire that ye should consider on the blessed and happy state of those that keep the

---

103. *Teachings of the Prophet Joseph Smith*, 255.

commandments of God. For behold, they are blessed in all things, both temporal and spiritual; and if they hold out faithful to the end they are received into heaven, that thereby they may dwell with God in a state of never-ending happiness (Mosiah 2:41).

John declared, "If ye know these things, happy are ye if ye do them." (John 13:17)

Members of the Church who live the gospel and missionaries who keep the mission rules are blessed and happy. Those who don't, aren't.

46

I had a mother who read the Bible to me

Abraham Lincoln once said, "All that I am or hope to be I owe to my Angel Mother."[104] I share the same sentiment for my mother.

As an infant, mom was abandoned by her single-parent birth mother and placed on a random doorstep in a baby basket. She spent many of her formative years in an adoption agency. Finally, she was adopted into the Jobe family. Mom said the Jobes were so poor that she brushed her teeth with a piece of rag with salt and soda on it. She only owned two dresses: the one she had on and another hanging in the closet, and she suffered from malnutrition. Yet my mother excelled in all things that she pursued. She was a straight-A student on every report card from the first grade through high school. She was the fastest runner in her school until the eighth grade. She could out-run any boy or girl. In fact, Mom said she used to chase boys she had a crush on home from school and beat the tar out of them. I asked, "Mom, why would you do that?"

She said, "Well, maybe then they'd notice me."

I'm sure they did.

Mom came out to California with mere nickels and dimes in her pocket and met my dad. Shortly thereafter they were married and started having pups. I was the runt of the litter.

I was told that I was two years old before my feet ever touched the ground because Mom carried me everywhere. Mom said she'd rather have the house a foot deep in dust than not to hold and squeeze and love her little Rusty. Truly she epitomized the statement of Joseph F. Smith, who said, "The love of a true Mother is nearer being like the love of God than any other kind of love."[105]

My mother made sure that her boys were raised Christian. We attended the Presbyterian Church in Arcadia, California. I greatly

---

104. Josiah Gilbert Holland, *The Life of Abraham Lincoln* (Springfield, MA: Bill Gurdon, 1886), 6.
105. Joseph F. Smith, *Gospel Doctrine*, 314–15.

admired our reverend, Dr. Barnard. I often thought, "When I grow up, I want to be just like him." Each summer in my childhood we went to Vacation Bible School. I remember singing "It's the B-I-B-L-E, That's the Book for Me," "Jesus Loves the Little Children," and "Jesus Loves Me This I Know, for the Bible Tells Me So." In our teen years, we went to the Presbyterian Church Camp every summer in Big Bear, California.

My Mom had a unique way of teaching her children. For example, one day she asked Dad to drive the family to "skid row" in downtown Los Angeles. We parked across the street from the Midnight Mission. Mom pointed out the "winos" and drug addicts stumbling down the sidewalk or leaning up against buildings drinking alcohol from bottles in brown paper bags. If they sat through a sermon, the mission provided them with one free meal a day. Mom said, "Life is made up of choices. These people made bad ones. I hope you boys make good ones." Then she said, "Okay, Ray, let's go." After this one–minute lesson, we returned to our home in Arcadia, forty-five miles away. Needless to say, I have never partaken of drugs or alcohol.

On another occasion Mom and Dad drove Rod, Randy, and me to the hospital where W. C. Fields died. He was a comedian and contemporary of Charlie Chaplin, Laurel and Hardy, and the Three Stooges. While parked across the street from this building, my mother said, "It was reported that just before W. C. Fields died, he was reading the Bible. A friend, upon entering his hospital room, remarked, 'I didn't know you were a religious man.' Whereupon W. C. responded with his quick wit, 'I'm not, I'm looking for a loophole.'" My mother said to us, "The Bible is the word of God and contains the truth. There are no loopholes. If you want to go to heaven, you need to live its teachings!" Then Mom said, "Okay, Ray, let's go!" More than sixty years later I remember every single word of her impactful messages, the expression on her face and the conviction in her voice.

When I was in the third grade, my mom was diagnosed with cancer. The cancer metastasized from her breast to her hip and finally to her brain. During those eight years of illness, she suffered excruciating pain and was mostly confined to her bed after the amputation of her right leg. Yet she never once complained.

Upon returning home from school each afternoon I went directly to her bedside and gave an accounting. Some of my happiest memories occurred when I could report to her, "I was elected class president today at school," or "I won a tennis tournament and here is my trophy," or "I got a C in algebra," which was a major accomplishment for me. Mom would extend her arms toward me, embrace me, lift me off the ground over her body and onto the bed next to her. As we continued to embrace, we would rub noses like the "Eskimoses." While looking into each other's eyes I told her about my day. There's no way I could come home from school and say, "Mom, I've been immoral and robbed a girl of her virtue," or "I decided to take drugs because some of my friends are doing it," or "I'm going to drop out of school and be a tennis bum." I just couldn't do these things because it would break her heart. I would be willfully rebelling against my mother and the Christian values she taught me. My love and respect for my mom kept me on the straight and narrow path. I tried earnestly to never disappoint her.

Mom kept the family Bible on the night stand next to her bed. I noticed that some of the words in her Bible were in red print. When I asked her why, she replied, "The red words were spoken by Jesus. They are the most important ones for you to learn and apply in your life." Nearly every day she would say to me, "I was reading the Bible today, and I came across a beautiful verse I know you will really like. May I share it with you?" From these precious moments in the scriptures with my mom, I developed a reverence for the word of God that was planted deep in my heart from childhood and that remains with me today.

> You may have tangible wealth untold;
> Caskets of jewels and coffers of gold.
> Richer than I you can never be—
> I had a mother who read to me.[106]

---

106. Strickland Gillilan, https://www.goodreads.com/quotes/241079-you-may-have-tangible-wealth-untold-caskets-of-jewels-and.

When I came home from school, I would often find Mom standing on her one leg in great pain, ironing my perma-press shirts. I said, "Mom, you don't have to do that."

She would say, "I want you to look and be your best."

When I was sixteen years old, I was in Kalamazoo, Michigan, competing in the National Junior Tennis Tournament. I received a letter from Mom. The writing was so scribbled that it was not legible. I knew something was terribly wrong, so I immediately boarded a plane and flew home. The cancer had gone to my mother's brain. But before she passed away, I told her, "Mom, so help me God, I'm going to live so you'll be proud of your son!" I have honestly tried to live up to that promise.

> The holiest words my tongue can frame,
> The noblest thoughts my soul can claim,
> Unworthy are to praise the name,
> More precious than all others.
> An infant, when her love first came,
> A man, I find it still the same,
> Reverently I breathe her name,
> The blessed name of mother.[107]

---

107. George Griffith Fether, "The Name of Mother," quoted in Thomas S. Monson, "Behold Thy Mother," October 1973 general conference.

47

"Elder Sill, what is your key to success?"

Years ago, Sterling W. Sill was a visiting General Authority at the Newport Beach, California, stake conference. I was invited to attend the luncheon Saturday afternoon with Elder Sill and the stake leaders. During the course of the meal, I inquired of him, "Brother Sill, what is the key to your success?"

He taught me a lesson that greatly impacted my life. Elder Sill answered, "I walk to work each day for exercise. In my pocket I have typed on a 3x5 card an edifying poem, quotation, or scripture I memorize that day."

He instructed me, "The Lord has counseled us to 'treasure up in our minds continually the words of life' (D&C 84:85); 'to seek ye out of the best books words of wisdom; seek learning, even by studying and also by faith' (D&C 88:118); 'let virtue garnish thy thoughts unceasingly, and the Holy Ghost shall be thy constant companion' (D&C 121:45–46); and, 'For as a man thinketh in his heart, so is he" (Proverbs 23:7)."

He informed me that he was committing to memory the most inspirational statements of the greatest men and women who ever lived, such as Jesus Christ, Joseph Smith, Ralph Waldo Emerson, Charles Dickens, William Shakespeare, Elizabeth Barrett Browning, and so on. He continued, "I not only enjoy reading the classics, but I want these golden nuggets of thought so indelibly impressed upon my mind that I can recall them at a moment's notice. In this manner, they become a part of me and their thoughts become my thoughts." He admonished me to go and do likewise, a challenge which I have accepted wholeheartedly.

48

Memorize one scripture a week

President Gordon B. Hinckley counseled us, "May I suggest that in our family night gatherings we make it a project to memorize one scripture citation a week pertinent to this work. At the conclusion of a year our children will have on their lips a fund of scripture which will remain with them throughout their lives."[108]

To help our children learn, apply, and share the doctrines of the gospel, I went through the standard works and carefully selected fifty-two scriptures for our family to memorize. To initiate our scripture-a-week program, we would recite a scripture before family prayer in the morning and again in the evening. We repeated the same reference every day for the week. As part of family home evening, we reviewed each of the scriptures we had memorized so far. This helped us retain what we had learned.

The fifty-two scriptures are listed below:

1. **Joshua 24:15:** Choose you this day whom ye will serve . . . but as for me and my house, we will serve the Lord.
2. **John 11:25:** Jesus said unto her, I am the resurrection, and the life: he that believeth in me, though he were dead, yet shall he live.
3. **Matthew 5:48:** Be ye therefore perfect even as your Father which is in heaven is perfect.
4. **Alma 41:10:** Behold, I say unto you, wickedness never was happiness.
5. **Mosiah 3:17:** There shall be no other name given nor any other way nor means whereby salvation can come unto the children of men, only in and through the name of Christ, the Lord Omnipotent.
6. **Hebrews 11:1:** Now faith is the substance of things hoped for, the evidence of things not seen.
7. **D&C 58:42:** Behold, he who has repented of his sins the same is forgiven, and I the Lord, remember them no more.
8. **John 3:16:** For God so loved the world, that He gave his only begotten son, that whosoever believeth in Him should not perish, but have everlasting life.
9. **John 14:15:** If ye love me, keep my commandments.

---

108. Gordon B. Hinckley, in Conference Report, April 1959.

10. **John 15:16:** Ye have not chosen me, but I have chosen you and ordained you.

11. **Matthew 16:19:** And I will give unto thee the keys of the Kingdom of Heaven: and whatsoever thou shalt bind on earth shall be bound in heaven.

12. **1 Nephi 3:7:** I will go and do the things which the Lord hath commanded.

13. **3 Nephi 18:20:** And whatsoever ye shall ask the Father in my name, which is right, believing that ye shall receive, behold it shall be given unto you.

14. **Proverbs 3:5:** Trust in the Lord with all thine heart; and lean not unto thine own understanding. In all thy ways acknowledge him, and he shall direct thy paths.

15. **Matthew 7:21:** Not everyone that saith unto me, Lord, Lord shall enter into the kingdom of heaven; but he that doeth the will of my Father which is in heaven.

16. **James 1:5:** If any of you lack wisdom, let him ask of God, that giveth to all men liberally, and upbraideth not: and it shall be given him.

17. **Matthew 5:8:** Blessed are the pure in heart, for they shall see God.

18. **Revelation 14:6:** And I saw another angel fly in the midst of heaven, having the everlasting gospel to preach unto them that dwell on earth, and to every nation, and kindred, and tongue, and people.

19. **Amos 3:7:** Surely the Lord God will do nothing, but he revealeth his secret unto his servants the prophets.

20. **Matthew 7:15–16:** Beware of false prophets, which come to you in sheep's clothing, but inwardly they are ravening wolves. Ye shall know them by their fruits.

21. **Matthew 6:24:** No man can serve two masters: for either he will hate the one, and love the other; or else he will hold to the one and despise the other. Ye cannot serve God and mammon.

22. **D&C 135:3:** Joseph Smith, the Prophet and Seer of the Lord, has done more, save Jesus only, for the salvation of men in this world, than any other man that ever lived in it . . .

23. **Malachi 3:10:** Bring ye all the tithes into the storehouse, that there may be meat in mine house, and prove me now herewith, saith the Lord of hosts, if I will not open you the windows of heaven, and pour you out a blessing, that there shall not be room enough to receive it.

24. **1 Corinthians 3:16–17:** Know ye not that ye are the temple of God, and that the Spirit of God dwelleth in you? If any man defile

the temple of God, him shall God destroy; for the temple of God is holy, which temple ye are.

25. **Exodus 20:7:** Thou shalt not take the name of the Lord, thy God in vain; for the Lord will not hold him guiltless that taketh his name in vain.

26. **Exodus 20:8:** Remember the Sabbath day, to keep it holy.

27. **Genesis 1:26:** And God said, let us make man in our image, after our likeness: and let them have dominion over the . . . earth.

28. **2 Nephi 25:26:** And we talk of Christ, we rejoice in Christ, we preach of Christ, we prophesy of Christ, and we write according to our prophecies, that our children may know to what source they may look for remission of their sins.

29. **Moroni 10:4:** And when ye shall receive these things, I would exhort you that ye would ask God, the Eternal Father, in the name of Christ, if these things are not true; and if ye shall ask with a sincere heart, with real intent, having faith in Christ, He will manifest the truth of it unto you, by the power of the Holy Ghost.

30. **D&C 14:7:** And, if you keep my commandments and endure to the end, you shall have eternal life, which gift is the greatest of all gifts of God.

31. **Moses 1:39:** For behold, this is my work and my glory, to bring to pass the immortality and eternal life of man.

32. **D&C 82:10:** I, the Lord am bound when ye do what I say; but when ye do not what I say, ye have no promise.

33. **Matthew 6:33:** But seek ye first the kingdom of God, and his righteousness; and all these things shall be added unto you.

34. **Matthew 7:12:** Therefore all things whatsoever ye would that man should do to you, do ye even so to them: for this is the law and the prophets.

35. **Matthew 22:36–39:** Master, which is the great commandment in the law? Jesus said unto him, Thou shalt love the Lord thy God with all thy heart, with all thy soul, and with all thine mind. This is the first and great commandment. The second is like unto it, Thou shalt love thy neighbour as thyself.

36. **Matthew 28:19:** Go ye therefore, and teach all nations, baptizing them in the name of the Father, and of the Son, and of the Holy Ghost:

37. **John 3:5:** Jesus answered . . . except a man be born of water and of the spirit, he cannot enter into the kingdom of God.

38. **John 17:3:** And this is life eternal, that they might know thee the only true God, and Jesus Christ, whom thou hast sent.

39. **John 14:6:** Jesus saith unto him, I am the way, the truth, and the life: no man cometh unto the Father, but by me.

40. **Alma 34:32:** For behold, this life is the time for men to prepare to meet God; yea, behold the day of this life is the day for men to perform their labors.

41. **John 14:2:** In my Father's house are many mansions: if it were not so, I would have told you. I go to prepare a place for you.

42. **1 Corinthians 15:21–22:** For since by man came death, by man came also the resurrection of the dead. For as in Adam all die, even so in Christ shall all be made alive.

43. **John 13:34–35:** A new commandment I give unto you, that ye love one another; as I have loved you, that ye also love one another. By this shall men know that ye are my disciples, if ye have love one to another.

44. **Mosiah 2:17:** And behold, I tell you these things that ye may learn wisdom; that ye may learn that when ye are in the service of your fellow beings ye are only in the service of your God.

45. **Romans 1:16:** For I am not ashamed of the gospel of Christ: for it is the power of God unto salvation to everyone that believeth.

46. **D&C 88:81:** Behold, I sent you out to testify and warn the people, and it becometh every man who hath been warned to warn his neighbor.

47. **John 8:31–32:** If ye continue in my word, then are ye my disciples indeed; And ye shall know the truth, and the truth shall make you free.

48. **Matthew 5:44:** But I say unto you, Love your enemies, bless them that curse you, do good to them that hate you, and pray for them which despitefully use you, and persecute you.

49. **John 14:26:** But the Comforter, which is the Holy Ghost, whom the Father will send in my name, he shall teach you all things, and bring all things to your remembrance, whatsoever I have said unto you.

50. **Matthew 7:14:** Because strait is the gate, and narrow is the way, which leadeth unto life, and few there be that find it.

51. **Matthew 10:39:** He that findeth his life shall lose it: and he that loseth his life for my sake shall find it.

52. **Ether 12:6:** Faith is things which are hoped for and not seen; wherefore, dispute not because ye see not, for ye receive no witness until after the trial of your faith

49

My testimony

Through the power of the Holy Ghost I have learned for myself that God is our loving Father in Heaven. We are His children, created in His image. Jesus Christ is the Son of the living God, our Savior and Redeemer, who atoned for our sins and overcame death by His glorious resurrection. He is the right way, the complete truth, and the abundant life. Jesus Christ is the only name under heaven whereby we may be saved. I know that the Father and the Son appeared to Joseph Smith and called him to be a prophet. Joseph received priesthood authority to restore the "true and living church" of Jesus Christ with the fullness of the gospel. Joseph Smith translated the Book of Mormon—Another Testament of Jesus Christ, by the gift and power of God. I know there is a divinely chosen living prophet of God on the earth today. Because of the priesthood keys administered in the temple which bind on earth and seal in heaven for time and eternity, our family can be together forever!

Russell N. Greiner, CES Institute Director, Memorized Scripture List

CHRIST
2 Nephi 9:41
2 Nephi 26:33
Omni 1:26
Mosiah 3:8
Mosiah 3:17
Mosiah 5:13
Helaman 5:12
3 Nephi 27:13–14
Ether 12:41
Moroni 10:32
D&C 19:23
Moses 1:39
Moses 6:63
Matthew 1:21
Matthew 11:5
Matthew 11:28–30
Matthew 18:20
Matthew 23:37
Luke 1:37
Luke 2:1–17
Luke 2:52
John 3:16–17
John 14:6
John 15:5
John 16:33
Acts 4:12
Romans 8:38–39
1 Corinthians 10:1–4
1 Corinthians 15:3–4
Philippians 2:9–11
Colossians 1:14–15
Hebrews 13:8
Revelation 1:8
Revelation 3:20
Exodus 6:2–3
Ecclesiastes 3:14
Isaiah 7:14
Isaiah 9:6
Isaiah 43:11
Isaiah 49:15–16
Zechariah 12:10

ATONEMENT
2 Nephi 2:6–7
2 Nephi 2:26
2 Nephi 9:21–22
2 Nephi 25:26
Mosiah 3:7
Mosiah 3:19
Alma 7:11–13
Alma 11:40–41
Alma 34:8–9
Alma 42:15
D&C 18:11–12
D&C 19:16–19
D&C 45:3–5
D&C 76:40–42
D&C 88:33
Luke 22:42–44
John 15:13
Romans 3:23–25
1 Peter 1:18–20
1 John 1:7
1 John 2:1–2
Isaiah 53:3–5

GRACE
2 Nephi 2:8
2 Nephi 10:23,24
2 Nephi 25:23
Titus 2:11–12

GODHEAD
3 Nephi 11:3, 6–7
D&C 130:22–23
John 5:19
John 8:17–18
John 14:8–9
John 14:28
John 16:27–29
John 17:3–5
John 17:20–22
Acts 7:55–56
1 Timothy 2:3–6
Hebrews 1:1–3

James 3:9
Genesis 1:26–27
Genesis 5:1–3

GODS
John 10:34–35
Romans 8:16–17
1 Corinthians 8:5–6
Philippians 2:5–6
1 John 3:2
Revelation 1:6
Genesis 3:22
Deuteronomy 10:17
Psalms 82:1, 6

PLAN OF SALVATION (PRE-MORTAL LIFE)
Alma 13:3
Ether 3:15–17
D&C 93:28–29, 36
Moses 3:5
Abraham 3:22–23
John 1:1–4,14
John 6:38
John 8:58
John 17:3–5
Acts 17:29
Ephesians 3:9
Ephesians 3:14–15
Colossians 1:14–15
Hebrews 12:9
Revelation 12:7–9
Numbers 16:22
1 Kings 22:19
Job 1:6
Job 32:8
Job 38:4, 7
Proverbs 8:22–23, 30–31
Jeremiah 1:4–5

PLAN OF SALVATION (VEIL)
1 Corinthians 13:12

Ecclesiastes 1:11
Isaiah 25:7

**PLAN OF SALVATION
(PURPOSE OF LIFE)**
2 Nephi 2:11
2 Nephi 2:25,27
2 Nephi 28:7–9
Alma 34:31–32
D&C 93:33–34
D&C 131:6
Abraham 3:25
Matthew 6:33
Matthew 16: 24–26
Romans 6:23
1 Corinthians 10:13
2 Corinthians 5:7
Galatians 6:7–9
Philippians 2:12
1 Thessalonians 5:21–22

**PLAN OF SALVATION
(SPIRIT WORLD)**
Alma 40:11–12
Luke 23:43
John 3:13
John 5:25
John 20:16–17
1 Peter 3:18–19
1 Peter 4:6

SECOND COMING
D&C 45:26–27
D&C 45:51–52
D&C 101:32–33
Acts 1:9–11
1 Thessalonians 4:16–17
Revelation 21:3–4
Malachi 3:1–2

**PLAN OF SALVATION
(RESURRECTION)**
1 Nephi 15:34
Alma 11:43–44
Alma 40:23
Alma 41:10
3 Nephi 11:7–15
D&C 88:15–16

D&C 130:2
Matthew 27:52–53
Matthew 28:1–8
Luke 24:1–9
Luke 24:36–39
John 5:28–29
John 10:17–18
John 11:25
John 14:1–2
John 20:26–29
Acts 1:3
Acts 24:15
Romans 6:9–10
1 Corinthians 2:9
1 Corinthians 15:5–6
1 Corinthians 15:20–22
1 Corinthians 15:40–42
1 Corinthians 15:44–45
1 Corinthians 15:55
2 Corinthians 12:2,4
1 Timothy 6:7
Revelation 20:6
Job 19:25–27
Ecclesiastes 12:7
Isaiah 26:19

**PLAN OF SALVATION
(JUDGMENT)**
1 Nephi 10:20–21
Mosiah 4:30
Alma 12:14,16
Mormon 9:4
D&C 72:3–4
D&C 76:111–112
D&C 121:29
D&C 137:9
Matthew 25:21
John 5:22
John 5:30
2 Corinthians 3:9
Revelation 20:12

FAITH
1 Nephi 7:12
1 Nephi 17:50
Jacob 4:6
Mosiah 4:9–10
Alma 30:44

Alma 32:21, 26–28
Alma 37:6
Ether 12:6
Ether 12:27
Moroni 7:33
D&C 88:118
D&C 90:24
Matthew 21:21
Mark 9:23
Romans 8:31
Romans 10:17
Philippians 4:13
2 Timothy 4:7–8
Hebrews 11:1
Hebrews 11:6
James 1:3
James 2:14–20,26
Joshua 1:9
Psalms 19:1
Proverbs 3:5–6

**CALLING &
ELECTION**
D&C 67:10–11
D&C 88:68
D&C 93:1
D&C 131:5
John 14:21
2 Peter 1:10

HOPE
Ether 12:4
Moroni 7:41
1 Corinthians 15:19

CHARITY
Moroni 7:47
Matthew 5:44
Matthew 7:12
Matthew 22:36–39
John 13:34–35
Romans 8:28
1 Corinthians 13:1–13
1 Peter 4:8
1 John 4:7–8
1 John 4:20–21
Deuteronomy 6:5–7

REPENTANCE

Mosiah 4:2–3
Mosiah 26:29–30
Alma 22:18
Alma 34:17
Alma 34:34–35
Alma 36:16–21
D&C 1:31–32
D&C 18:10,13–14
D&C 58:42–43
Luke 9:62
2 Corinthians 7:10
Philippians 3:13–14
Hebrews 6:6
2 Peter 3:9
1 John 1:7–9
Psalms 51:10–11
Proverbs 28:13
Isaiah 1:18
Isaiah 43:25
Ezekiel 18:21–22

BAPTISM

2 Nephi 9:23–24
2 Nephi 31:4–12
2 Nephi 31:13
2 Nephi 31:17
Mosiah 18:8–10
Alma 7:14–15
3 Nephi 11:33–34
3 Nephi 27:19–20
Ether 4:18–19
Moroni 6:2–3
Moroni 8:25
D&C 20:37
D&C 20:73–74
D&C 22:1–4
D&C 84:74
Matthew 3:13–17
Mark 1:4
Luke 3:3
John 3:5
Acts 2:37–38
Acts 8:12
Acts 8:36–38
Acts 19:1–6
Acts 22:16
Romans 6:3–5

Galatians 3:27
Colossians 2:12

INFANT BAPTISM

Moroni 8:10–12,20
Moses 6:54

BAPTISM FOR THE DEAD

D&C 128:22
1 Corinthians 15:29

HOLY GHOST

1 Nephi 4:6
1 Nephi 10:17
1 Nephi 17:45
2 Nephi 32:5
2 Nephi 33:1–2
Jacob 4:13
Mosiah 2:9
Mosiah 5:2
Alma 10:6
Helaman 5:30
Moroni 7:16–19
D&C 6:22–23
D&C 8:2–3
D&C 9:7–9
D&C 11:12–13
D&C 63:64
D&C 76:12
D&C 84:85
D&C 85:6
Matthew 10:20
Luke 24:32
John 14:26
John 14:27
Acts 8:14–17
1 Corinthians 2:11–14
Galatians 5:22–23
1 Kings 19:11–12
Joel 2:28

ENDURE TO THE END

2 Nephi 31:16
2 Nephi 31:19–20
D&C 14:7
D&C 81:6

Matthew 24:13

BORN AGAIN

Mosiah 5:7
Mosiah 27:25–26
Alma 5:14–16, 26–27
Alma 7:14
Moses 6:59–60
John 3:3–5
1 John 5:4–5
Ezekiel 36:26–27

PRAYER

1 Nephi 15:8–9
2 Nephi 32:8–9
Enos 1:4
Alma 37:35–37
Helaman 3:35
Helaman 10:4–5
3 Nephi 18:18
3 Nephi 18:20
3 Nephi 18:21
3 Nephi 19:9
Mormon 9:27
Moroni 7:9
Moroni 7:48
D&C 9:7–9
D&C 10:5
D&C 25:12
D&C 46:30
D&C 50:29–30
D&C 88:63–65
D&C 101:7–8
D&C 112:10
Matthew 6:9–13
Matthew 7:7–8
Matthew 21:22
James 1:5–6
James 4:3
James 5:16
1 John 3:22
Numbers 6:24–26
Psalms 23:1–6
Proverbs 21:13

GRATITUDE

Alma 26:16
D&C 78:19

D&C 136:28
1 Thessalonians 5:16–18
Psalms 118:24

APOSTASY
Alma 24:30
Joseph Smith History
1:19
Joseph Smith History
1:21
Matthew 15:8–9
Matthew 21:43
Acts 20:29–30
1 Corinthians 1:10–14
Galatians 1:6–8
2 Thessalonians 2:1–3
1 Timothy 4:1–3
2 Timothy 3:1–7
2 Timothy 4:3–4
2 Peter 2:21
Jude 1:10
Deuteronomy 4:28
Isaiah 24:5
Isaiah 30:9–11
Isaiah 60:2
Amos 8:11–12

RESTORATION
D&C 1:29–30
D&C 13
D&C 27:12–13
Joseph Smith History
1:5–8, 11–15, 16–17
Matthew 17:11–13
Acts 3:20–21
Ephesians 1:10
Isaiah 11:12
Isaiah 29:13–14
Daniel 2:44–45
Malachi 4:5–6

BOOK OF MORMON
1 Nephi 6:4
1 Nephi 13:40
2 Nephi 3:12
2 Nephi 29:3,8
2 Nephi 33:5
2 Nephi 33:10–11

Moroni 10:3–5
D&C 17:6
D&C 20:5–12
D&C 84:57
John 10:14–16
3 Nephi 15:21
2 Corinthians 13:1
Revelation 14:6–7
Genesis 49:22–26
Deuteronomy 4:2
2 Kings 19:31
1 Chronicles 5:1–2
Psalms 85:11
Isaiah 29:11–12
Isaiah 29:17–19,24
Ezekiel 37:15–17

PROPHETS
2 Nephi 3:14–15
Jacob 7:11
D&C 1:14,17
D&C 1:38
D&C 5:10
D&C 20:25–26
D&C 21:4–5
D&C 35:17
D&C 68:3–4
D&C 76:22–24
D&C 122:1–2
D&C 135:3
Moses 1:11
Joseph Smith History
1:25
Matthew 7:15–16
Matthew 10:41
Mark 2:22
Luke 24:25
1 Corinthians 9:1
Hebrews 9:16–17
Revelation 19:10
Genesis 17:1
Genesis 32:30
Exodus 24:9–11
Exodus 33:11
Numbers 11:29
Numbers 12:6–8
Deuteronomy 18:18
2 Chronicles 20:20

Isaiah 6:1,5
Jeremiah 28:9
Amos 3:7
Malachi 3:1–2

REVELATION
2 Nephi 28:29–30
Jacob 4:8
Alma 5:46
Mormon 9:7–8
D&C 42:61
D&C 50:24
Matthew 16:15–18
Acts 1:1–2
1 Cor 12:3
Galatians 1:11–12
Ephesians 3:3–5
Job 33:14–16

**PRIESTHOOD
& CHURCH
GOVERNMENT**
Jacob 1:19
Mosiah 18:17
Alma 4:10
3 Nephi 8:1
3 Nephi 27:7
3 Nephi 27:8
3 Nephi 27:21
Moroni 6:4
D&C 6:6
D&C 13
D&C 26:2
D&C 27:12–13
D&C 42:11
D&C 42:42
D&C 43:8–9
D&C 64:29
D&C 81:5
D&C 82:14
D&C 84:33–41
D&C 105:5
D&C 107:18–19
D&C 107:99–100
D&C 108:7
D&C 115:4
D&C 121:33–46
Moses 7:18

Matthew 10:5–6
Matthew 15:24
Matthew 16:19
Mark 3:14–15
Luke 6:13–16
Luke 10:1,17
John 15:16
Acts 1:22–26
Acts 2:47
Acts 6:6–8
Acts 8:18–20
Acts 10:34–35
Acts 13:2–3
Acts 19:1–6
Acts 19:13–16
1 Corinthians 11:2
1 Corinthians 12:27–31
Ephesians 2:19–20
Ephesians 4:5
Ephesians 4:11–14
Ephesians 5:23
Titus 1:5
Hebrews 5:4–6
Hebrews 5:8–10
Hebrews 7:11–12
James 5:14–15
1 Peter 2:9
Exodus 40:12–13
Numbers 27:18–19

COMMANDMENTS
TEN
COMMANDMENTS
Exodus 20:3–17

CHASTITY
Jacob 2:35
Alma 39:5
Alma 39:11
Moroni 9:9
D&C 42:22–25
D&C 59:6
1 Corinthians 6:9–10
1 Corinthians 6:19–20
Proverbs 6:32
Proverbs 12:4

SABBATH
D&C 59:9–10
Exodus 20:8–11

TITHING
D&C 64:23
Malachi 3:8–10

WORD OF WISDOM
D&C 89:18–21
1 Corinthians 3:16–17

JUDGING
Moroni 7:16–19
Matthew 7:1–5
1 Samuel 16:7

COMMANDMENTS
(GENERAL)
D&C 29:34–35
D&C 88:121, 123–125
Psalms 19:7–8

OBEDIENCE
1 Nephi 3:7
1 Nephi 17:3
2 Nephi 9:28–29
Jacob 4:10
Mosiah 2:41
Mosiah 5:5
Alma 7:23–24
Alma 37:35
Alma 57:21
D&C 14:7
D&C 58:21
D&C 59:23
D&C 64:34
D&C 82:3
D&C 82:10
D&C 84:44
D&C 130:20–21
D&C 132:5
Moses 5:6–8
Abraham 3:25
Matthew 5:3–12
Matthew 6:22
Matthew 7:13–14
Matthew 7:21–23

Luke 6:46
John 7:16–17
John 13:17
John 14:15
James 1:22
1 John 2:3–4
1 Samuel 15:22
Ecclesiastes 12:13
Isaiah 64:8

SERVICE
Jacob 2:18–19
Mosiah 2:17
Mosiah 2:21–22
D&C 42:29
D&C 58:26–28
D&C 59:5
D&C 76:5–6
D&C 98:13
Matthew 6:24
Matthew 7:12
Matthew 10:39
Matthew 23:11–12
Matthew 25:40
Luke 6:38
Acts 10:38
James 1:27
1 Peter 2:15
Joshua 24:15

MISSIONARY
WORK
1 Nephi 13:37
Mosiah 28:3
Alma 6:6
Alma 17:2–3
Alma 17:16
Alma 26:11–12
Alma 26:22
Alma 29:1–2
Alma 29:8
Alma 29:9
Alma 31:5
Alma 31:34–35
Alma 36:24
Alma 38:10–12
3 Nephi 5:13
3 Nephi 7:18

D&C 1:4–5
D&C 4:1–7
D&C 6:9
D&C 11:20–21
D&C 12:8
D&C 14:8
D&C 15:6
D&C 18:15–16
D&C 19:29–31
D&C 27:15–18
D&C 29:7
D&C 31:5
D&C 33:7–10
D&C 34:6–10
D&C 35:13–14
D&C 42:6–7
D&C 43:15–16
D&C 50:13–14
D&C 52:9
D&C 58:47
D&C 58:64
D&C 60:13
D&C 63:37
D&C 63:58
D&C 84:88
D&C 84:106
D&C 88:81–82
D&C 90:11
D&C 100:5–8
D&C 103:36
D&C 112:19
D&C 123:12–13
Matthew 9:37–38
Matthew 19:29
Matthew 24:14
Matthew 28:19–20
Mark 6:7–12
Mark 16:15–18
Luke 22:32
Acts 1:6–8
Acts 5:38–39
Acts 6:10
Romans 8:31
Romans 10:15
1 Corinthians 3:6
1 Corinthians 9:16–18
James 5:19–20

Jeremiah 3:14
Jeremiah 16:16

TESTIMONY
Alma 5:45–46
D&C 60:2–3
D&C 62:3
D&C 76:79
Matthew 10:32–33
John 6:66–69
John 7:16–17
John 8:31–32
Romans 1:16
1 Corinthians 12:3
2 Timothy 1:7–8
1 Peter 3:15
Revelation 3:15–16
Revelation 19:10

EXAMPLE
2 Nephi 31:9
Alma 48:17
3 Nephi 12:48
3 Nephi 18:24
3 Nephi 27:27
Matthew 5:14–16
Matthew 5:48
John 13:15
1 Timothy 4:12

SCRIPTURE STUDY
1 Nephi 1:12
1 Nephi 15:24
1 Nephi 19:23
2 Nephi 4:15
2 Nephi 32:3
Helaman 3:29
D&C 1:37
D&C 6:2
D&C 18:34–36
D&C 68:3–4
John 5:39
John 20:31
John 21:25
2 Corinthians 3:3
2 Timothy 3:16–17

2 Peter 1:19–21
Joshua 1:8
Psalms 119:103
Psalms 119:105
Isaiah 30:8
Jeremiah 20:9
Jeremiah 31:33

EDUCATION
D&C 90:15
D&C 93:24
D&C 93:36, 53
D&C 130:18–19

TEACHING
2 Nephi 33:1
Mosiah 23:14
Alma 31:5
Alma 38:10–12
D&C 42:12
D&C 42:14
D&C 50:21–23
D&C 88:77–78
D&C 88:122
Acts 8:30–31
Romans 2:21
Romans 10:14
Ezra 7:10

SACRAMENT
Moroni 6:5–6
D&C 20:77,79
Luke 22:19–20
1 Corinthians 11:23–30

TEMPLES
D&C 88:119
D&C 97:15–16
D&C 109:22–23
Psalms 24:3–4
Isaiah 2:2–5

MARRIAGE & FAMILY
Mosiah 4:14–15
3 Nephi 22:13
D&C 49:15

D&C 49:16
D&C 68:25
D&C 93:40
D&C 131:1–3
D&C 132:19–20
Mark 10:6–9
Mark 10:14
1 Corinthians 7:3
1 Corinthians 11:11
2 Corinthians 6:14
Ephesians 5:25
Ephesians 6:4
1 Timothy 5:8
3 John 1:4
Genesis 18:19
Proverbs 18:22
Proverbs 22:1
Proverbs 22:6
Proverbs 31:10–11, 26, 28

THOUGHTS
2 Nephi 9:39
Mosiah 4:30
Alma 12:14
D&C 6:36
D&C 84:85
D&C 121:45–46
Proverbs 15:26
Proverbs 23:7
Isaiah 55:8–9

FORGIVENESS
D&C 64:9–10
Matthew 18:21–22
Luke 6:37

SELF-DISCIPLINE
Matthew 18:3
Romans 12:21
Ephesians 4:26
Ephesians 4:31–32
James 1:8
James 1:19
Proverbs 15:1
Proverbs 16:18
Proverbs 16:32
Proverbs 25:28

UNITY
4 Nephi 1:15–17
D&C 38:24,27
Moses 7:18
Mark 3:23–25

AMERICA
Mosiah 29:26–27
Ether 2:12
Matthew 21:43
Proverbs 14:34
Proverbs 29:2

ADVERSITY
Alma 36:3
D&C 58:3–4
D&C 121:7–8
D&C 122:7–8
D&C 136:31
Romans 5:3–5

SIN/DISOBEDIENCE
3 Nephi 6:18
D&C 59:21
D&C 82:7
Titus 1:16
Hebrews 10:26
James 4:17
1 John 3:4
Proverbs 6:16–19
Isaiah 5:20
Hosea 8:7

DEVIL
2 Nephi 28:20–22
3 Nephi 11:29
D&C 10:27
Moses 4:4
Revelation 12:7–9
Revelation 13:7

**ARTICLES
OF FAITH**

Acknowledgments

Special thanks to my wife, Dianne, for her loving encouragement to produce the manuscript; my celestial secretary, Sherri Bewsey, for typing the material; and the professional team at Cedar Fort Publishing for making this project a reality.

About the Author

Russell N. Greiner was born in Arcadia, California, and raised a Christian. He served in student government and played a variety of sports. In high school he played number one on the tennis team and was the undefeated league champ. He was awarded a tennis scholarship to the University of Redlands. In 1971 Russ helped his team win the NAIA National Championship and became an All-American. He then received a tennis scholarship to Brigham Young University. While at BYU, he was baptized a member of The Church of Jesus Christ of Latter-day Saints by his missionary, teacher, mentor, and friend, Ed J. Pinegar. Following his mission to Montana–Wyoming he graduated from BYU and married his sweetheart, Dianne Boden, in the Los Angeles Temple. They are blessed with three married children and twelve adorable grandchildren.

Russ taught thirty years in the seminary and institute program of the Church. He has served in a variety of Church callings, including Young Men's president, elders quorum president, ward mission leader, stake mission president, high councilman, bishop, counselor to three mission presidents, and temple ordinance worker. He has been a speaker at Especially for Youth, Education Week, the BYU Religion Symposium, and many youth and young adult conferences and firesides. He is the author of *The Truth of the Matter.*

Scan to visit

www.russgreiner.com